TO: CONNIE
FROM: CHRISTOP
"THE PSYCHOLOGY GUY"

LOOK FOR GOOD IN LIFE!

It's Not Rocket Surgery

How to be a Star Leader at Every Level

Christopher J. Irelan, PhD
& Julie L. Irelan

SECOND RIVER
HEALTHCARE PRESS

It's Not Rocket Surgery
How to be a Star Leader
at Every Level

Second River Healthcare Press
26 C Shawnee Way
Bozeman, MT 59715

Phone (406) 586-8775
FAX (406) 586-5672

Editor: Diane Dannenfeldt
Cover Design: Christopher R. Jackson
Cover Art: Roger Schillerstrom
Cover Layout: Lan Weisberger
Typesetting/Composition: Neuhaus Tyrrell Graphic Design

Irelan, Christopher & Irelan, Julie It's Not Rocket Surgery: How to be a Star Leader at Every Level / Christopher J. Irelan, PhD, Julie L. Irelan

ISBN-10: 0-9743860-7-3 (hard cover) ISBN-10: 0-9743860-8-1 (soft cover)
ISBN-13: 978-0-9743860-7-2 (hard cover) ISBN-13: 978-0-9743860-8-9 (soft cover)

1. Self Help 2. Leadership 3. Motivation

Library of Congress Control Number: 2007940832

First Printing July 2008

TABLE OF CONTENTS

DEDICATION

To our Connor and our Kelsey, you are the reason that we do what we do—never, ever lose the Power of Perspective!

To Jerry Pogue and Chris Jackson, our publishers. Without your patience, constant insight, faithful reminders, and gentle redirects, this book would never have become a reality—here's to many more!

To Laurie Evans, MSW, thank you for helping me find my LAURI. It is your insight that made this dream come true. May this book be an inspiration to others as much as you have been to us—you are truly a professional's professional.

INTRODUCTION

Have you ever noticed someone who is a leader in any capacity and asked yourself either, "Why them and not me?" or "How did they get there?" If you are like most people who have asked these questions, you probably have a pretty standard list of answers. They were born leaders. They had the right education. They knew the right people. They had the right doors opened for them. They were in the right place at the right time. They were lucky. They come from a family of leaders. They are more intelligent than others. They were destined to be leaders.

There are countless answers that you can give as to why certain people are leaders. Perhaps some of these answers are true. Maybe even more than one applies to them. Even so, none of those answers, or any like them, make a truly effective leader effective. Many times individuals have several of the answers listed in the paragraph above presented to them, yet they still are not effective as leaders. What then is it that makes successful leaders successful? The answer is simple and any one of us reading this book can use it to become an effective leader.

The answer is a simple three part formula that literally anyone can use to achieve amazing results and become a *Star Leader at Every Level.* This entire book is based on this formula that we call The Personal Excellence Formula™.

1. Effective leaders DETERMINE WHAT THEY WANT out of life.
2. Effective leaders DECIDE TO TAKE MASSIVE ACTION.
3. Effective leaders DISCIPLINE THEMSELVES to take that action.

It's a simple three part formula that anyone can begin to do today, right now, and begin achieving amazing results. This is the reason why we wrote this book. We want to show you how simple it is to be an effective leader in any area of your life. This is also the reason why you need to read this book, in its entirety.

The truth is that successful leaders are just like you and me. You don't have to make it any harder than it needs to be. You simply need to do the three things of the Personal Excellence Formula™. It is not complicated, in fact as we have said, it is really quite simple.

So what is the only basic requirement to being an effective leader? Is it fate? Is it coincidence? Is it knowing the right people? Is it going to the right schools? Is it coming from the right family? No. The answer is none of these. The only basic requirement to being an effective leader is SELF-DISCIPLINE.

With self-discipline, literally anyone can do the three steps of the Personal Excellence Formula™. In fact, you have already started in the right direction! By picking up this book, you have begun to determine what it is that you really want out of life. You have determined to learn what it is that effective leaders have in common. More than that, you have decided to at least examine what this star leadership is all about. Congratulations! It will only get easier from here. You have already taken two of the three steps. This separates you from the rest and includes you in a class with the most successful leaders of any field.

You can take this another step farther. Decide right now that you will finish reading this entire book. It is an easy read and contains some entertaining and downright funny stories. The stories serve the purpose of explaining or applying the basic truths of effective leadership that any of us can both relate to on some level and apply in our lives for outstanding results, starting today!

CHAPTER 1

BRAIN SURGERY AND ROCKET SCIENCE

MAKING OUTSTANDING PROGRESS IS EASIER THAN YOU MAY THINK

So why does this book have "*Rocket Surgery*" in the title? Because if you look at brain surgeons or rocket scientists, the chances are that you will find that they are not any more gifted, lucky, or blessed with the "right timing" than you or me. While their fields of study are considered complicated or highly intellectual by many individuals, the truth is that they are not. The reality is that individuals in these fields, like many other areas of life that people consider out of reach, have simply disciplined themselves to the three basic steps of the Personal Excellence Formula™. They have:

1. DETERMINED what they want out of life.
2. DECIDED to take massive action to realize those goals.
3. DISCIPLINED themselves to take massive action and stay the course.

Allow me to explain through two actual interactions that I experienced.

BRAIN SURGERY

This past summer, our family was enjoying a Milwaukee Brewers baseball game. We watched as Geoff Jenkins cracked a line drive, allowing both Bill Hall and Prince Fielder to score and giving the Brewers a two-run advantage.

Turning to the woman on my right, I commented, "That was a great play! Our family loves coming to Brewers' games!"

"This is our first one," she replied with a smile of enjoyment and enthusiasm and eyes as wide open as a small child overwhelmed with excitement at a state fair. "Does your family come to many of them?" she asked.

"We sure do," I replied. "We are season ticket holders."

"Wow! You are serious fans!" she said, still watching with amazement the cheering fans that nearly filled Miller Park that day.

"We are! Very much so!" I agreed. "But we also do personal excellence training for the Brewers sales staff. They're fun clients to work with."

"Personal excellence training. That sounds like fun! Is that about becoming better at what you do?" she inquired.

"Exactly! It is all about becoming better at what you do because you are better at being who you are and all that you can be. A lot of people don't understand this connection—or they understand it but don't put it into practice. It is fun to see people actually learn how to improve their thoughts, actions, and relationships to achieve incredible and amazing results!"

I introduced myself, Julie, and our kids, and she introduced herself as Beverly and her husband, Thomas. They seemed like really great people who were enjoying a slice of Americana at the ballpark.

We continued to talk between cheering on the Brewers and rooting for our favorite players. At one point in the conversation, she asked me, "So is your work very difficult or complicated?"

"Well, yes and no," I responded.

"What do you mean by that?"

"Well," I replied, "those are two different categories. The concepts that we teach can completely change the progress, success, and outcomes that individuals are able to achieve, but those concepts take discipline. That is the difficult part. But the concepts themselves are not that complicated."

"What do you mean?" she asked with such genuine interest that she stopped watching the game and turned to me.

"You see, Beverly, getting people to want to take action requires them to ask questions in two important areas:

1. Am I completely satisfied with my life? Am I who I want to be? Am I where I want to be? Do I have what I want to have? Have I achieved all that I have dreamed I could achieve?
2. If not, what is stopping me or holding me back? Am I willing to think about things just a little differently to have massive and positive outcomes? And if so, where do I begin?

Helping people see what they can be, do, and have is easy. It is not exactly brain surgery. The difficult and challenging part is for them to take ownership of making progress and want to find the application for their life."

"That makes a lot of sense," she replied. "Brain surgery is only difficult if you choose to make it that way. If you choose to make it simple, it more or less is. Disciplining yourself to the years of school and the constant learning curve is challenging and takes commitment. However, once you master that, the rest is as difficult or easy as you make it.

"A field like that, or any other challenge, may seem overwhelming at first, but if you keep your focus and take it one step at a time, you are able to accomplish far more than you initially thought. The more you practice, the easier it becomes. Soon you are doing it on a regular basis and others are amazed at what you can do. But they didn't see your determination to learn it and your discipline to master it. Ultimately, you have proven to yourself that you could do it, and each time you do what you do, you remind yourself of what you are capable of."

"That is a great example," I said in amazement. "Where did you come up with it?"

"I am a brain surgeon," she said with a confident and friendly smile while turning back to watch the game.

What a great attitude Beverly has. She is living the principles that we teach and want to share with you in this book. She believed in what she could do, and that belief has allowed her the freedom and confidence to live a life of personal excellence. She also understood the fundamental principles of high-performance leadership—that passion and drive are the most important components in achieving your desired outcomes.

ROCKET SCIENCE

That ballpark conversation reminded me of a similar one ten years earlier. I was at a golfing event for a non-profit organization for which Julie and I served as consultants. I was paired with Steven whom I had known professionally for a few years. Steven and I spent the day together golfing and enjoying the beautiful weather and the well-designed and superbly manicured golf course.

"This would be a nice club to join," I remarked as we pulled up to the third hole.

"Yeah, must be nice," Steven said sarcastically.

"Have you ever thought of joining it?" I asked.

"That's funny," he retorted with a friendly and familiar sarcasm.

"Why?" I asked, suspecting what the answer would be based on my knowledge of Steven and his self-limiting attitude.

"You have to have money and connections to join a club like this," he stated emphatically. "Neither of which I have now or foresee having."

What a limiting and self-defeating prophecy, I thought to myself. As we continued to golf, I learned more about the limiting personal and professional situation that the "fates of life" had cast on him and in which he found himself helpless and captive, like a starfish in a fishing net. Even the golf course seemed to be against him because I, a new golfer, was outscoring him, a veteran golfer of twenty-plus years, on every hole.

As we continued to golf, I asked him a series of questions to determine why he was not nearly as successful as he could be. Why didn't he have a better position? By better, I mean in terms of job satisfaction and professional value in his mind, not in terms of money or title. In other words, why did he feel stuck personally and professionally?

I wanted to ease him into thinking about it. I did not want to venture down the pathway of "passion" and "drive" as that was light-years ahead of his thought process. I decided, from my years of experience as a coach and consultant, to meet him where he was and at the speed at which he was accustomed to living.

I stood there and let him swing. As the ball hooked to the left and launched deep into the woods, he commented, "Figures." I handed him a beverage as I joined him. I put my arm around his shoulder, squeezed it, sighed, and said, "Steve, do you like what you do. I mean, are you...happy?"

"What kind of a question is that?" he asked, as if he questioned whether anyone is really happy with their career, life, or self.

As we continued to talk, he droned on about the "lukewarmness" of his life, about others' opportunities, and about how things come so easily to some people. As he placed his club back into the golf bag with all of the emotional constitution of a soggy pastry, I began to understand.

"So do you have any siblings?" I inquired at a subtle place in the conversation.

"Ha," he said as he pulled the cart forward. I had let him drive so he could feel some sense of control in his life.

"My younger brother 'Ted,'" he said, making quotation marks in the air with his fingers while he said "Ted" in the tone of a third-grader who had just been kicked off the swings by the sixth-graders.

"What does he do?" I asked, inevitably knowing it would be something that, from Steven's perspective, positioned his brother as the boy-wonder in not just his parent's eyes, but the eyes of perhaps the entire free world.

"Are you ready for this one?" he said with a disgusted snicker.

"Sure, hit me," I responded.

"He is a rocket scientist. I mean the real deal. He is actually a r-o-c-k-e-t s-c-i-e-n-t-i-s-t," he said, enunciating every letter slowly so I would get the impact of what he was saying.

Have you ever wanted to laugh at something but couldn't because it would be inappropriate? I almost popped a gasket trying not to laugh. Instead, I sipped my soda and turned to the outside of the cart, pretending to enjoy the breeze. It was not Steven that I was laughing at. It was how two people can come from the same house, the same background, and the same opportunities—and one ends up happily chasing stars with rockets while the other is taking personal offense at an inanimate object.

Luckily for me, Steven started talking so I had time to try and regain my composure…which was not easy as I observed him glare into the hated woods while screeching the golf cart to a halt that made me rock like a human Weeble Wobble. He got out and grabbed his golf club like one of Arnold Schwarzenegger's characters getting a gun while dressed in camouflage. What made it worse was that he had on sunglasses like Arnold's and was holding a cigar in his mouth with the same determination, while possessing the body of Don Knott's character Barney Fife from *The Andy Griffith Show.*

Thank you, Lord, was my only thought; *you've given me a legitimate reason to laugh*!

I burst into laughter and immediately said, "Wow! You look like Arnold Schwarzenegger loading up for a kill."

With all the seriousness he could muster, he said, "I've had it. Those woods have stolen my ball for the last time." Turning to go in search of his ball, he tripped and fell face first. Luckily, the only thing injured was his pride. I could not help it....I burst into uncontrollable laughter and said, "You're too much, Steve! You are just too much!" At that point, we both started laughing at the ridiculousness of the situation.

As we continued to talk and golf, it became evident to me why I outscored him as a new golfer and why his brother—with the same background, education, experiences, and opportunities—was a successful rocket scientist while Steven was unhappy. Steven had a self-defeating attitude, settled for average instead of designing his destiny, and had not developed passion or drive. I found it interesting that both brothers had struggled mightily to achieve and maintain good grades in school. They both had to make what I call the decision of determination. Ted had made it. Steven had not.

Ted had failed on three important tests to become a rocket scientist and had to retake each one after lengthy studying and review. Finally, after an indescribably difficult mental and intellectual effort, he passed the tests. Steven had not scored high enough on his college entrance exams to get into the first two schools of his choice. While he could have retaken the exams, he chose to settle for the third school on his list. This, by the way, was a far less prestigious school whose diploma would offer him less status and opportunity than the first two. However, it was his choice. He chose to settle. After all, settling is far easier to do than striving. But while settling may be an easier decision up front, the frustrating and mediocre outcomes can be much harder to live with.

Rocket Surgery

As we begin this journey of exploring personal excellence with you, we remind you to think of the words of Beverly, the brain surgeon: "A field like that, or any other challenge, may seem overwhelming at first, but if you keep your focus and take it one step at a time, you are able to accomplish far more than you initially thought. The more you practice, the easier it becomes. Soon you are doing it on a regular basis and others are amazed at what you can do. But they didn't see your determination to learn it and your discipline to master it. Ultimately, you have proven to yourself that you could do it, and each time you do what you do, you remind yourself of what you are capable of."

By now it should be obvious why this book is called *It's Not Rocket Surgery.* Many people view rocket science and brain surgery as fields that are too overwhelming or complex to undertake. The truth is that the individuals in those professions took steps of personal excellence by believing they were capable of meeting the challenge. Your journey of personal excellence does not need to seem overwhelming or daunting. It is not rocket science or brain surgery. Rather, your journey is simply one of decision.

High-performance leaders in any field of study or personal undertaking all started with one thing: a decision. Decisions are what change lives and create progress. Each of us makes decisions every day as part of life. We can choose to make decisions based on ease, or we can make them based on excellence. We invite you to join us and others who we continue to coach and train in making decisions based on excellence. We invite you to have and achieve all that you desire and deserve. The opportunity is here for your taking. Your new and exciting future awaits you! Let's get started!

Chapter 2

Is Your Glass In The Dishwasher?

Simple Choices Make A Big Difference

Many people describe a person as an optimist or pessimist based on whether they see a glass as half empty or half full. This way of looking at things has been around for quite a while, and it is a useful way to explain and understand the concept. To understand personal excellence, however, we think that you must ask a different question: *"What is in your glass?"* You see, no matter whether a glass is half empty or half full, its contents are going to determine if you are happy as a leprechaun or sour as a grape.

About a year ago, our family was sitting in our kitchen on a Saturday, taking a break from mixing play and chores. Yes, we still call them chores. Remember, we do live in Tennessee. Anyway, we decided to have lunch to refuel for more fun and work. We made the sandwiches, poured our drinks, and sat down to relax. I love milk. It is my favorite beverage in the world, so I poured a large, full glass of pasteurized, homogenized, vitamin D added milk. (It used to just be called "milk." Ah yes, lawyers and marketers.)

We sat down, joked and giggled, started the forbidden food fight when Julie was not looking, and enjoyed each other's company and the love we share as a family. Okay, so Julie turned around during the food fight. Like I said, the "love" we share. Forgive and forget and all that. Anyway, that is when *it* happened and I will never forget…

One of our projects that Saturday was finishing the new countertop we had just put in. We had just finished placing some ceramic tiles that came from a local construction project fifty years ago. Although the building was built in 1956, they had literally thousands of leftover tiles. As a result, we acquired them at a very reasonable price. We planned to use them to make a one-of-a-kind countertop for our counters and the island in the center of our kitchen.

A friend of ours is the head of maintenance at Concordia University Wisconsin, where Julie and I attended college. Our friend explained that the tiles needed to be sealed to maintain their shine, luster, and strength. He was kind enough to provide us with a gallon of commercial-grade, extra-strength floor sealer that the university purchases in vast quantities. Before lunch, we had been using that sealer to finish the counter by sealing the tiles. I had just poured a full glass of it when we broke for lunch. It had a white, milky look and not much smell.

As you can probably imagine already, while I was eating my lunch, I got up to grab my milk off the island and took the wrong glass. To this day, I don't know how I picked up the wrong glass. It was not even one of our regular drinking glasses but an old one that we used for such projects.

Anyway, because milk is my favorite beverage, I took a big mouthful and filled my cheeks like a growing third-grade boy in the school cafeteria. Without swallowing, I instantly knew something was drastically wrong. I had never felt this sensation before, and I never want to feel it again. I don't know quite how to describe it, but every single cell in my mouth felt instantly "tightened." They felt...well..."sealed."

Your mind is an amazing thing. When your body is in perceived or real danger, your mind can instantly make comparisons to pictures that it has seen. I kid you not; with my cheeks full and a growing, almost explosive feeling in my mouth, I was picturing an atomic bomb and a mushroom cloud. I felt like my mouth was shriveling at the same time the sealer was expanding.

I immediately ran from the room at what looked like

lightning speed to Julie and the children, but in my mind, it took forever. I felt like a slow-motion television character when the film is slowed down to show him running really slowly and he speaks with a slower and much lower voice to indicate the prolonged nature of the situation. I could hear myself thinking (insert slow, low television voice), *Nooooooo! Muuust get toooo theeeee bathroooom*!

As I spit out the sealer in the sink, two phrases kept echoing relentlessly in my mind: *Commercial Grade* and *Extra Strength*. My mouth was "sealed," for all practical purposes. It was shiny. I used water and rinsed, but there was no difference. The sealer is water insoluble unless extremely diluted. Therefore, one glass of water won't dilute it, no matter how hard you rinse. I rinsed and rinsed and rinsed. I used mouthwash. I brushed my teeth four times. I used more mouthwash. I used glass after glass of water. Slowly, over time, it began to wear off.

My initial audio response was to yell out "Ohhhh, yuuuck!" with such comedic force that my family burst into uncontrollable laughter upon realizing both what had happened and that I was all right. Julie's response through laughter was, "Are you all right?" My daughter commented, "Daddy, your teeth look really shiny," and my growing athletic son added, "If you're not going to finish your sandwich, can I have it?" Julie was creative enough to write "Do not ingest" and "Not for human consumption" on the sides of the glass in black marker.

From that time forward, I have approached my beloved milk with the apprehension of someone trying something for the first time. I look at it. Smell it. Look at it again and s-l-o-w-l-y take a sip.

My story proves a simple point. It was not how full or half empty my glass was. I only had one mouthful. It was what was in the glass that counted. It was not milk. It was tile sealer. It works great on floors and counters, but not so well on humans. So, when you talk about seeing life as a glass half empty or half full, you need to ask yourself if that is really what is important.

Is it more important to ask yourself, "What is in my glass?" We think it is. It may not be the quantity of certain things in your life that matters but the quality. In other words, it may not be how much or how little of something you have. Instead, it may be the value or positive nature of what you have, or quite frankly, the negative nature.

Negative things, even in small quantities, are negative. They become like a poison that can literally make you sick. Negative thoughts, negative self-talk, and negative feelings about yourself or your situation in life can all serve, even in small quantities, as poison. They can begin to erode slowly or quickly at the happiness that you desire and deserve.

I only got a mouthful of tile sealer, but if I had swallowed, I have no doubt I would have felt ill. I would have had to go to the doctor or hospital and have them pump my stomach or give me something quickly to counteract the sealer's effect. It was only a small amount, but it was poisonous to put into my body. In much the same way, your thoughts, your self-talk, your self-image, and your interactions and relationships with others can be a destroying poison, even in small quantities, if they are negative.

To begin your journey of personal excellence, decide right now that you will not allow these things in your life. Julie has a wonderful phrase that she has used for many years. She has taught our children and me this phrase, as well as countless others whose lives she has positively affected. She says, "When it comes to your thoughts about you, you cannot afford the luxury of a negative thought."

Isn't that beautiful? Isn't that powerful? Let us examine briefly why that is. If you have a negative thought about yourself, in any area of your life, you open a door that you cannot afford to (and should not) open. That one thought—that one negative interpretation of yourself as a physical, emotional, intellectual, and spiritual being—opens the door for a changing mindset. Thoughts are incredibly powerful. Words are merely thoughts that are spoken or written. They have a powerful effect.

What if, instead of "allowing the luxury of a negative thought" in examining what is in your glass, you start with a positive affirmation? An "affirmation" is really just stating that something is true. It says it is a reality. When I drank tile sealer, I could have said, "See, it figures. I always do things like this." I could have said, "Boy, am I stupid." I could have said, "Chris, you are such an idiot." But I did not. Instead, after the "Noooo mussst finnnnd bathroooom!" and the, "Ohhhh, yuuuuuuck!" my thoughts were, *Wow! I cannot believe I did that! I am usually really observant.* I did not judge myself. I did not even judge my actions. I simply made an observation, nothing more.

If we are going to examine what it means to be on a journey of personal excellence to become a leader at every level, we must first understand personal excellence itself. That means first understanding ourselves and then understanding others. The process is simple when you break it down that way. Simple, you ask? Yes, remember the book is called *It's Not Rocket Surgery.* In this book, we are going to examine many of the concepts, ideas, thoughts, and ways of looking at yourself and the world that your mother may have taught you but that we forget as we get older.

Our starting place is looking at our glass. Recently, I was giving a speech to about three hundred people, and we were speaking about the question of what is in your glass. During the question-and-answer period, one woman stood up and said, "What if you don't have a glass?" I joked and asked her if that was her own question or from the voices in her head, which made her and everyone else burst into laughter. Then I addressed her question.

"Everyone has a glass," I explained. "By being alive, we each have a glass. We each have our own way of looking at ourselves and at others. But how we look at others will largely be a reflection of how we see ourselves. Saying it another way: Our glass is simply our view first of ourselves and then of how we connect with others."

As I went on to explain, I could see faces begin to light up. I could see their eyes begin to clear. I watched as members of the audience who had never looked at it this way before began to understand the power and impact of positive affirmations. They suddenly began to realize that how they thought and talked about themselves would determine and affect how they thought and talked about others. What you say about yourself is what others believe.

In other words, others will take your negative words as true. What you say in a moment of frustration could be heard by others as a moment of truth. We all want things in life. Are we the reason we are not getting them? Are we accidentally sabotaging our own successes by entertaining even the slightest negative thought about ourselves?

The world will show you products and try to make you believe that you are not whole without them. This is only marketing and not done because you truly need them. The world will continually tell us that we are inadequate. This is not to put us down, but to sell us things to make us feel better. But we'll never feel better if we don't start from the inside.

Negative thoughts are like getting into a boxing ring and finding out you are the only one fighting. Each negative thought that you allow is like a punch thrown at you…BY YOU. There will never be a winner because you are allowing yourself to be influenced in a negative way. That affects your happiness in life by affecting how you feel about yourself and how you interact with others.

At another speaking engagement, a member of the audience asked jokingly, "What if your glass is in the dishwasher?"

I replied, "Then you have to ask yourself if the timer is set to wash it soon or if the light is on to indicate the dishes are clean." The audience laughed, as did I, but I went on to explain my point. When I asked if the glass was waiting to be washed or if the all-clean sign was lit up, I was speaking about a metaphor for life.

It all comes back to the concept of "what is in your glass." If you are carrying around past events that you see as failures or missed opportunities, you need to clean out your glass, so to speak. You need to realize that the past is the past and that, in many cases, there is no good or bad and no failures or successes. In many cases, you simply have opportunities to learn and celebrate that you are much further along, smarter, more experienced, or stronger than you were before that experience.

Everyone has a drop-off point or bottom of the hole. The bottom of a hole is reached when you stop digging. People take a while to understand this point. When is enough enough? Recognize that reaching the bottom is not the end, just the beginning of your journey out of a situation. Even after the worst event, you must choose to focus on either the negative that occurred or the positive that is coming. You might not have had a choice while the event was happening, but you certainly have a choice afterwards to stay negative or to clean out your glass and start over. When my back was broken as a result of someone else's negligent driving, I had two choices. I could feel sorry for myself and keep feeling like a victim, or I could put what happened in the past and move on. I chose the second.

When you go to a wine tasting, you cleanse the palate between selections to prepare to truly experience the taste and texture of the next wine. Life is the same way. Life is a series of experiences. If we are to truly experience the good in our glass, we need to make sure that the glass is clean. In the example of my becoming the "human tile" and drinking from the wrong glass, once I realized that the glass contained tile sealer, I didn't just add milk. I switched glasses. Perhaps you need to do the same thing, metaphorically speaking.

Perhaps you have had negative relationships in the past, or a negative self-image, or what you perceive to be a failure in business or something else. If so, switch glasses. Tell yourself that the negative relationship was simply a learning experience with the type of person that you do not want to be with. If you had a negative self-image, ask yourself why. Most likely, you'll discover that someone else started you on that negative self-image and you simply chose to accept it and adopt it as your view. Perhaps it started with a negative comment, or several negative comments. Maybe the person let you down repeatedly or was dishonest with you. Or maybe you weren't included in a group when you wanted to be. No matter what the event or interaction was, the negative self-image was someone else's view, not yours.

This leads to a really important point regarding what is in your glass. You can chose to adopt what others said about you, felt about you, or did to you—or you can chose not to. If you go along with them, you're taking what is in their glass and putting it in yours! Think about that for a minute. Because they do not have a great self-image, they may be projecting onto you how they feel about themselves.

Remember, this book is about personal excellence as it leads to high-performance leadership. In studying this, we have found an irrefutable truth: How you feel about yourself will determine how you feel about others and interact with them. Bringing this simple and effective concept full circle, if you have a negative view of yourself or feel inferior or deficient in any way, someone who you admired or respected, consciously or subconsciously, probably reflected on you how they really felt about themselves.

So what do we do, or I should ask, what did I attempt to do? In my story, my goal was to drink milk to go with my sandwich so I would have enough energy and strength to finish the counter and have fun with my family. The milk would give me strength to make proper use of the sealer. Instead, I was careless and unfocused and put the wrong liquid in my body. I can look back and laugh now; actually I was laughing at the time, too. The same concept applies to you. There are three truths that we need to be aware of in life.

First, you are in control of what you put in your glass. Are you putting in positive thoughts about yourself? Are you listening when others compliment you and point out your strengths? Do you note the things that you feel you do right or do best? Do you review your accomplishments and successes? I invite you to accept and own only those thoughts and expressions from others that will build you up, strengthen you, and fill your glass with what you both desire and deserve.

Second, if you carelessly surround yourself with people, concepts, and situations that are less than positive, you'll experience the concept of drinking tile sealer by accident. I did not intend to drink tile sealer, and I did not enjoy it. I was careless, and I paid a price. Thankfully, the price was only an awful taste, shiny teeth, and lost appetite. If I had swallowed the sealer, it would have become part of me temporarily, and I would have had to seek professional help to deal with its poisonous consequences.

The same thing applies with our glass of life. If we are careless and surround ourselves with harmful people, concepts, and false information, their negative ideas temporarily become a part of us. That can hurt us physically, emotionally, and spiritually. Then, as we too often see, we need to seek professional help to deal with the poisonous concepts and avoid an even more negative outcome.

So what do we do? We avoid being careless. *I am not saying to be defensive and keep a constant guard up.* Quite the opposite, I am saying to surround yourself with positive people, concepts, and situations whenever possible. Surround yourself with people and environments that will allow you to be the wonderful person that you are and accept you for who you are. This is a safety net.

Listening seriously to any negative word, comment, view, or expression about you has no place in your way of thinking. In the immortal words of Don Knott's character, Barney Fife, from *The Andy Griffith Show*, you must "Nip it in the bud!" One negative word or phrase, one thought or expression, can lead to another and another. If you listen, before long, you'll develop a negative self-image or a cynical, negative view of life. This leads to our next important point.

Third, what you do with what is in your glass determines the level of personal excellence you will achieve. As we just discussed, you are in control of your glass and its contents. You have to be careful and not be reckless with what you put in it. Now that we understand those two concepts, what do we do with the contents of our glass? We invite others to share in it with us.

In my example, had I grabbed the right glass, I would have had a glass filled with milk. Then, if Julie, our son, or our daughter had asked me for some, I could have shared it. Obviously I would not want to share the sealer with them because I care about them. Applied to our lives, are we putting the right things in our glass? Are we being careful vs. careless? Are we sharing only what is good and positive?

As we look throughout this book at personal excellence, let's keep in mind the concept of the glass of life. Let's ask ourselves what we are putting in that glass. Let's ask ourselves if the contents are good for us or will get us where we want to be. Personal excellence is not a destination; it is a journey! It revolves around our decisions and our actions. It means connecting our thoughts and actions today with our outcomes and opportunities tomorrow. Personal excellence starts with our vision for happiness. And that begins with looking inside and accepting and liking who we are.

Here is the best part: If we don't like something about ourselves, we can change it! But that change must begin with the inside. Too many times, we have seen people make outward changes—altering their hair color, their eye color with colored contacts, their weight by dieting and exercising, or their skin tone by tanning. None of these changes are bad, but many of these people remain miserable because they did not start by changing inside. If weight loss were the answer to happiness, all models would be happy. Obviously, not all of them are.

In our journey of personal excellence, we must first change our *internal representations.* That is to say, we must change how we feel about us, at the gut level. We must remove any negative feelings about who we are or what others may have said about us. Remember, what others say about you is simply their view based on what is in their glass, or how they feel about themselves.

I don't know whether you have a negative view of yourself or not. I am simply saying that you need to remove any negative feelings that you have about yourself, even if they are few and far between. Stop looking at what you could have done in a situation or what you should not have done. That situation is over, and life is about today and tomorrow.

I am not saying to pretend something negative didn't happen. If you ask someone to marry you and they say no, don't go looking for a place to host your reception dinner. That's called denial. I also am not saying to pretend that something great happened when it did not. For example, don't go out and buy an expensive car on credit because you just won the lottery when you haven't even bought a ticket. That, too, is called denial of reality.

I am simply saying that situations are what they are. Review and learn from them, but don't dwell on them. You cannot go back and change a situation, so why beat yourself up over it? If you have ever seen a two-year-old screaming for candy in a grocery store, you know emotions can get the best of us. Don't let your inner-child react to situations in life like that. Simply look for the good! If you look for it, you generally will find it.

Two years ago, an acquaintance of ours kept referring to the past and how she felt she had been mistreated. It was true that her parents had not treated her in the way most of us think loving parents would. This person did two things in response. First, she constantly tied her self-worth to how she had been mistreated. She placed a value on herself based on how someone else chose to treat her. Second, she began to believe this view of herself with such conviction that she expected others to treat her the same way, and she developed an emotional defense mechanism. She would not allow herself to get close to many people because she expected to be emotionally hurt or mistreated.

I remember this clearly because I recall Julie gently sharing with this individual that she had two choices. She could look to the past and dwell on a situation that she could not change, or she could look to the beauty of today and expect good things to take place. Julie explained that if this person reviewed all the positive things about herself and then her positive interactions with others, she could plan on good things happening today and tomorrow.

Julie suggested that this person give herself daily positive affirmations. Julie taught her that the more often she did this, the more solidified these core truths would become and the more clearly she would make these concepts a reality in her life. Soon, life would become a journey of eager expectation.

I would like to finish this chapter by sharing the personal affirmations that Julie suggested. I would also like to suggest that you consider making these affirmations a part of your thought process beginning today.

Positive Personal Affirmations

Personal Affirmation One: I am special and unique. This is not a new concept, but it might be for you. Stop for a moment as we begin this journey of personal excellence and consider that you are a one-of-a-kind, living miracle. Only you have the genetic makeup that you have. Only you have your exact combination of abilities, talents, emotions, thoughts, and feelings. Take time to celebrate that! Do not let anyone else's opinion change your idea of who you are. You were created special and unique. You have a wonderful opportunity to give back to this world as only you can and to experience the joy and peace that you deserve. Starting today, celebrate you!

Personal Affirmation Two: I am in control of my happiness. You were created to live life to the fullest and celebrate all that is wonderful and precious about being alive. You deserve to be happy. If you are not, you have allowed someone or something to get in the way. Years ago, when we were living in Oklahoma after graduate school, I was doing private consultation with a senior woman that I'll call "Ellen."

Ellen had been married for forty-three years when her husband "Bill" died. She began to focus on the loneliness and self-inflicted misery that she was experiencing instead of on the good years with him. She told me that she could not be happy without Bill. I asked her if she thought that Bill would want her to be sad, now that he was gone, or happy for the time they had together.

"Ellen," I said. "What if Bill was here right now with us in this room? What do you think he would say to you?"

"I don't know," she responded.

"Yes, you do, Ellen," I gently encouraged. "You were married forty-three years, and you knew him better than anyone else. What do you think he would say?"

"I think that he would say he wants me to be happy."

"Do you think he would tell you that you deserve to be happy and that you are special and wonderful?"

"Yes, I do," she said, grinning as her glazed eyes pictured the face of her late husband. "Yes, I think that is exactly what my Bill would say."

"Well, Ellen," I gently inquired, "What is stopping you from being happy?"

"My loneliness and the fact that I miss him so much."

"Ellen, you deserve to be happy. You were a wonderful and dedicated wife for many years. Bill would want you to enjoy your twilight years thinking about all of the good times that you had and the love that you shared."

"But I just keep thinking about the things I could have done differently or better while he was alive," she offered.

"Will thinking about that bring him back or change the past?" I asked.

"Well...no," she realized in open honesty.

"Then, why don't you focus on what you can control, namely, today and tomorrow. You deserve to be happy. Give yourself that permission and that foundation as a truth to live by today and tomorrow."

I asked her to affirm this daily in her mind. Over time, I saw her outlook and attitude change. I saw her happiness increase, and the smiles on her face become real. She could not bring back her beloved Bill, but she assured herself daily that she was in control, not of him being alive or deceased, but of her reaction to the good times that they shared. For you, the reader of this book, please realize that you—not others, not circumstances, not situations—are in control of your happiness. Start today by reviewing what is great about your life!

Personal Affirmation Three: What I look for, I will find. What you think about, you will look for. And if you look hard enough, you'll find what you look for. What are you looking for? What are you focusing on? Share with yourself that whatever you want to receive and experience in life is where you will focus your positive mental energy. If you look at the cover of this book, you'll see that the artist has drawn a person with a big smile and twinkling eyes who is riding the rocket of life to the realization that he is a star.

You are a star!

Start to realize that today. Start to internalize it, and watch incredible miracles take place in your life. Why will they take place? Because you are looking for them. As you look for them, you'll begin to see exciting opportunities. They were right in front of you before, but you weren't looking for them. Start by looking for the great things within yourself.

As I said before, you are a unique and special person. The more that you begin to celebrate this, the more you will bring this positive energy into your thoughts, your actions, and your interactions. That positive energy will draw others to you and create virtually limitless opportunities. You will begin to experience the life that you desire and deserve. Start telling yourself that you will only allow positive thoughts to enter into your consciousness!

Personal Affirmation Four: There is no limit to what I am capable of. I don't know if you like dogs or not, but bear with me because Julie and I love dogs and have two—a pedigreed German Shepherd and a "medium" American Eskimo. He is two pounds into the medium class, but he still looks like a miniature. Shhhhhh...Don't tell him he's small; he thinks he is huge! That is the point of this example.

When we bring home new bones for the dogs to chew on, they each get one. Dogs being dogs, they like each other, but each of them thinks, "Don't touch my bone!" If our German Shepherd even walks by "Mr. Personality," as I call the American Eskimo, he growls and lets out a warning bark that says, "Don't even think about it sister!" He honestly has no clue that, with one swat, she could send him flying. He just knows that this is his bone, and he is willing to take on a dog five times his size to protect what he wants. Ironically, even though she could floss her teeth with him, the German Shepherd walks away, wonders, "Geeesssh, what is his problem?" and goes back to her own bone.

You and I can learn a lot from our American Eskimo. I'm not suggesting that you bark and growl the next time you go to a nice restaurant and the server brings your food. I'm not suggesting that while others enjoy dessert, you gnaw relentlessly on your bone. That's just wrong on so many levels. I also am not suggesting that you walk up to the table next to you and give the strangers the "puppy dog look" while looking at their food, then at them, then at their food, then back at them. Rather, what we can learn is to diligently pursue what we want or believe in, regardless of the apparent obstacles in our way.

Let me use a couple of human analogies to demonstrate my point, in case you are not into dogs. If Michael Jordan, the now retired basketball player, had let the murder of his father take over his thinking, he would never have played again. However, he knew his father would want him to, and so he persevered, played, and was absolutely amazing. Tiger Woods, the famous professional golfer, did the same thing, as did Brett Favre the quarterback for the Green Bay Packers, after the death of their fathers.

I use these three examples because the loss of someone we love can be emotionally paralyzing. Having someone important to us move away can be as painful as losing a spouse or anyone else in our life through death or divorce. On a completely different level, it can be painful to lose a job or a business contract.

Many things can throw us off track—from words from others to the loss of something or someone important in our life. However, they can only throw us off track if we let them. Each of us has the ability to overcome any of these things. There are countless examples of individuals who have overcome adversity. I know, from my own experience and from studying countless others, that nothing is out of your reach. *You simply need to believe in what you are capable of!* Start by taking a "no limits" attitude towards life, telling yourself that anything is possible. Start by taking that one small step in the direction of your dream, and feel the power of believing.

Personal Affirmation Five: I have a special purpose. You exist for a reason! Whether you believe that we evolved from apes or were created by an all-powerful God, the unchangeable truth is still the same. You are alive! You exist! You are taking up space in this world. You have a purpose. You are here on this planet at this time, in your form, to do something. Ask yourself what that is.

Some people go through life without realizing they have a purpose, and that's a tremendous waste. People who do realize their purpose live with passion, zeal, and fire in their bellies. They get up in the morning excited and enthusiastic because they are not simply existing. They are living!

Remind yourself that you have a purpose. If you don't know what it is, ask yourself what you are passionate about? What do you care about? What do you spend your time thinking about? As long as it's good and positive and not harmful to yourself or other people, maybe that's the purpose that you should pursue with passion. Tell yourself that you have a purpose and believe it! You have as much right to the job, relationship, or experience you want as the next person, so go get it! Pursue it will all your might. It won't magically come to you, so take action.

Practice these affirmations daily, and watch miracles begin to manifest themselves in your life. Watch good things start to happen. Watch negative things begin to diminish. I do not mean that negative things will go away, but they will have less power and impact on your life. By practicing these affirmations daily, you'll continue on your journey to develop personal excellence. Remember, simple choices in how we choose to look at life make a big difference in the quality of life that we experience.

CHAPTER 3

LIFE TAKES TURNS; TAKE THE STEERING WHEEL

PERSONAL EXCELLENCE IS AVAILABLE RIGHT NOW

This chapter is probably unlike anything you have read on goal setting. We have seen countless seminars, charts, computer programs, and day planners that supposedly can assist you with goal setting. They may or may not. One thing is for certain: If you do not take ownership of your goals, you have little chance of reaching them. Even if you do, reaching them will probably be a difficult task and not much fun. In this chapter, I want to share how I came to see goal setting from a new perspective that literally changed my life.

Julie and I met when we were in college. I was a junior. She was a freshman. I had to take an elective to fill three credits. Since I was already taking three foreign languages and several other advanced-level classes, I wanted to take a class with little or no homework. I had taken eighteen credits a semester during my first two years and had also signed up for eighteen each semester of my junior year. I wanted to take fewer credits my senior year so I could relax and enjoy my last year of college before heading to graduate school. So, here I was taking a choir class at Concordia University Wisconsin. It made sense. After all, there was no homework, and it was a fairly easy three credits.

On the first day of class, I was sitting in the third row from the bottom in the fifth chair from the right. I looked down and saw my future. At least I hoped she was. Julie was sitting in the first row in the fifth chair from the right. She was beautiful. Even more than that, it was literally love at first sight, something that I had never believed in. I fell instantly in love. It was much more than just physical attraction. There was chemistry. There was a synergy. There was something about her that told me she felt and thought very much like I did.

I leaned over to my close friend David Oberdieck and said, "I don't know anything about her, but if that girl will marry me, I want to spend the rest of my life with her."

Many people would laugh at this. Many people would blow it off and think you were being foolish, but not David. In the past year, David had taught me more about life and true happiness than any friend my age had ever done. David is a six-foot-six Texan who transferred to Concordia a year earlier to play football and study to be a Lutheran minister. He is a great guy. He is the real deal. David did not laugh at me or think I was foolish.

"So, what are you going to do about it?" he asked, bending down to whisper in my ear.

"I don't know yet. First I need to find out her name," I responded. "Then I'll find out what her hobbies are and see which match mine. I'll find some way, some excuse, and some activity that we have in common that will allow us to spend time together."

"You could just ask her," he said while elbowing me.

"No. It has to be more pre-planned than that," I retorted. "It has to seem natural."

"What's so unnatural about asking?" he asked.

"Nothing, I just have to make sure I set it up the right way. This is really important, and I don't want to blow it. I just don't want to take any chances," I said.

"You are a pretty pre-planned guy," he said with a chuckle. "If you want to go out with her that badly, you'll find a way."

During that class, I said, "Hi," and gave her a flirtatious smile as we practiced. Okay, so maybe I gave her several flirtatious smiles. I thought she was really beautiful, all right? Over the next several days, I began to notice the people she associated with. This was easy to do because Concordia University was a small, private university and we both lived on campus. Your chances of accidentally running into someone were good. Your opportunity to make it happen on purpose was even better, if you used the right strategy.

Being an outgoing guy who finds it easy to talk to just about anyone at any time, I soon found many opportunities to interact with her friends. I would casually slip into the conversation that I thought their friend Julie was beautiful and that I would love to get to know her better. I didn't want to be so covert that she wouldn't hear about it. After all, I didn't want her going out with someone else while I was planning.

Two days after I first saw her, I made it a point to run into one of her roommates, Stacy, who was working on a paper in the library. I sat down at the computer beside her.

As I began to boot up the program I needed, I casually said, "So, Stacy, your roommate is beautiful." As soon as I said it, I realized that was like telling a neighbor who had just bought a new car that the neighbor up the road had "a *really* nice one."

"Don't get me wrong; it's not that you are *not* beautiful. I just think that your roommate is gorgeous." This was not getting any better. Being good on my feet, I punted.

"Did you know that my next-door neighbor, Brad, thinks you are really cute?" I offered with one hand grasping for a blade of grass as I dangled emotionally over the open grave of unintended conversation.

"Really? I think he is cute, too."

"Then it's settled. I'll tell him to ask you out before somebody else does."

"You would do that?" she asked.

"Sure, Stacy. Anything for you," I offered with the genuine sarcasm of someone who had leapt out of the grave dressed in a football uniform, holding the ball with one arm straight out and headed for the fifty-yard line.

"I'll talk to Brad today," I assured her. "I want to get to know Julie, and I'm trying to figure out what she likes. What is she into?"

"That's easy," said Stacy without even taking her eyes off the computer screen or slowing as she typed her paper. "She's passionate about running."

Noooooo! I thought to myself. I had just been blindsided by a linebacker and knocked back to my own fifteen-yard line.

"What else is she into?" I asked in eager desperation.

"Running. That's what she loves. That's what she does."

Nuts! I thought to myself so loudly it would have drawn everyone's attention in the next two rooms if I'd said it out loud. I had been a judo instructor for more than ten years. I was a wrestler for six years. I had been racing bicycles for the last seven years. I was on a national bicycling team. Riding fifty miles was a cakewalk, a day at the park. It was nothing. It got me energized. I loved it.

Running was a different story. I couldn't run to the mailbox without getting as winded as a mechanic with a two-pack-a-day habit. It was all psychological. I was the team captain of the cycling team. I loved to ride and was in excellent cardiovascular shape. But my mind told me that I was not a runner.

"So," I said calmly, clearing my throat, "she's a runner, huh?"

"Completely and totally," she affirmed. "Ran cross-country all through junior high and high school. Oh, there is one other thing she likes."

Halleluiah! I internally exclaimed. *You're back in the game, baby*!

"She likes swimming. She's been a competitive swimmer since she was a little kid."

I heard the announcer's voice in my head as I felt temporarily set back. *Running to the twenty-, thirty-, forty-yard line, he's on a roll. No, wait. The other team is picking him up and carrying him back to his own end-zone. Forty, thirty, twenty, ten, five. They have placed him in his own end-zone. We have a turnover*!

Swimming?

Why me, Lord? I silently asked. I had taken swimming lessons as a child. When I was eight, I fell out of an inner tube in six feet of water while an inattentive instructor flirted with another instructor. I nearly drowned. I remember it as clear as a bell. I am a swimmer now, but only because I set my goals to become one. That, too, will play a part in this chapter on goal setting.

I felt as though I were flipping a coin. Running or swimming? Let's see. I want to cross the road, but do I want to chance getting hit by a bus or a semi? Let's see, bus or semi? Bus or semi? Bus or semi? It really does not matter. The question is: How badly do you want to get to the other side of the road?

"Okay, that's great," I said to Stacy. "I'm a much better runner than swimmer," I confidently proposed. "I'll ask her to go running."

How bad could it be? I thought to myself. *A guy my age can easily recover from a heart attack. It won't be that bad.*

Just to be sure, I asked her other friends the same question throughout the next day. It was a no-lose situation. She would know that I liked her by how many people I asked. In addition, perhaps I could win the lottery and find out that she liked something less conducive to cardiac arrest or physical endangerment. But every one of her friends said the same thing. Running and swimming.

Great, I thought to myself. *She might as well be into skydiving without a parachute.*

You're going down, I said to myself.

No. No, you're not, I answered. *How badly do you want to reach your goal?*

Okay, I'll do it, I assured myself. *But when the paramedic is yelling "Clear!" with the little paddles on your chest, just remember I warned you.*

Later the next day I saw her. I told her that I heard she liked running and found that a total coincidence because I liked it, too. In fact, I planned to go running that evening.

"Would you like to join me?" I asked.

"I would love to!" she answered.

(Insert sports announcer voice.) *Holy cow, folks, can you believe that? He throws for a ninety-nine yard pass, and it's complete! Touchdown! Chris Irelan, six points. Everyone else, zero*! (Insert video of end-zone victory dance.)

I walked back to class not even minding that my life might end within hours. She'd agreed to spend time with me, which was all that mattered. That concept consumed my thoughts through the rest of the day.

That evening, I got ready to go running. As I left my dorm room, I passed several guys in the hallway. I was on my way out, and they were just returning.

"Hi Chris," said Jeff. "Are you going to the gym to go lifting?" I was into lifting weights and still enjoy it.

"No. I'm going running!" I said confidently while waiting for the laughter to ensue.

Three, two, one... I counted down to myself.

All at once, all five of them started laughing in a friendly way as if to say, "You jokester, you."

"That's funny," said Jeff. "No, really. Where are you going?"

"I'm going running," I responded.

David was with the group and said, "You must have asked her, didn't you?"

"I sure did, and she said yes!"

"Who?" they all asked at the same time, but they were half a second off from each other.

"A new girl named Julie," David answered on my behalf.

"Is she that cute little blonde who lives in the Wartburg dorm?" one of them asked.

"That would be the one," I said with the confidence of a new pick for the NFL draft.

I headed out the door and walked over to Julie's dorm. She met me where we planned, right on time. It was evening, and the stars were shining. The autumn air blew gentle and warm off Lake Michigan. Julie was dressed in a navy-blue, silk runner's tank top, runner's shorts, and runner's shoes that looked lighter than air.

"I'm ready; let's go."

"Don't you want to change first?" she asked. "I didn't realize that you didn't have time."

"I did change." I was wearing a navy-blue, long-sleeved sweatshirt over a white Nike t-shirt. I was also sporting full-length, heavy cotton, blue sweatpants and the New Balance leather high-tops that I used for weight lifting.

"You're going to run in that?" she asked with genuine interest and disbelief.

"Oh sure," I said with the confidence of a game-show contestant who just gave a winning answer. "I do it all the time. It makes me stronger," I said as I jogged in place and rotated my neck like a boxer about to enter the ring. "That way, when I wear my actual running gear, swoosh, I can really go." I said as I turned to look forward, putting my hand out in front to simulate a blazing runner.

"Okay," she said with hesitation and continued disbelief.

We began to run. By the time we hit the entrance to the campus and were about to turn onto the road, I was already breaking into a mighty sweat. We ran the thirty yards to where the road becomes Lake Shore Drive. Lake Shore runs exactly two miles from Concordia University to Mequon Road, where you must turn left or right. It is exactly two miles back. As we ran, she heard my breathing and said, "Wow, you breathe heavily when you run!"

"Gasp...Yes...gasp...I know...I get more oxygen that way...gasp...It's good for you. It gives me a competitive advantage...gasp."

My feet were hitting the concrete with the same flapping sound as someone running in swim fins. My head was too far back and my chest was pushed disproportionately forward like a marathon runner who had just completed twenty-six miles.

About a half-mile into the run, I asked if we could stop.

"I...I have a rock in my shoe. I need to get it," I said bending over to pant like an asthmatic in a forest fire.

A few minutes later, as I thanked the Lord that I was still among the living, I said, "Okay...let's go," and made grunting noises like someone warming up for a big event. As we ran, I was breathing heavily enough to counteract the night breeze and suck the tree branches in my direction when I inhaled. I was sweating like someone crawling through the desert in search of water. With my swim-fin feet slapping the pavement and my chest flung out, I was, in fact, pathetic.

"You, uh, aren't really a runner, are you?" she honestly inquired.

"What makes you say that?" I asked.

"Everything," she said laughing.

"Nopers. Not really."

"Not really?" she said. "Kinda like an elephant isn't really a fish?"

"Something like that," I said through barely audible pants and gasps.

She wasn't stopping. She was giggling.

"Then why did you suggest running?"

"Gasp…pant…wheeze...Because I hate swimming."

She burst into laughter but never broke her stride. I continued to pant and never hit mine.

"I just...GAASSPP... wanted to...GAASSPP... spend some..... WHEEEEZE...time...GAASSPP... with you...GAASSPP."

"Well, in that case, let's spend some time together," she said as she increased her pace with what seemed to be the speed of a dragster leaving the starting line. Meanwhile, I was certain I could hear the defibrillator being loaded into the rescue unit.

I will never forget that night. She liked me but wanted to see if I was the kind of person she could see herself being with. She is a woman of high goals who gets the job done, yet she is also compassionate and gentle. She made me prove myself that night. She also paid me back for lying to her. She ran the entire two miles down and the entire two miles back. I was somewhere between being in heaven wanting to be with her, and thinking that I was dying and heading to heaven for real. The moon ahead of us was a combination of the romantic glow seen by two people in love and the bright-white light that beckons someone who is dying.

Oddly enough, as we ran and I heard her voice, I began to get a stride. All right, as much of a stride as a non-runner in heavy sweats and high-tops can get. I wanted my goal and my outcome badly enough that no temporary inconvenience, pain, or in this case, near-death experience, could dissuade me. I wanted to date this girl, even if it meant her standing over my coffin as I lay there in inappropriate non-runner's gear. I was not giving up.

We made it back, alive. I felt an exciting bliss. This was partly because my legs were numb and also because I had come to know her over those four agonizing miles and truly had fallen in love. I also felt bliss because my goal setting had pushed me to do something that previously seemed impossible. I wanted my outcome so badly that I was willing to literally run through the pain, doubt, and disbelief to hit my goal.

We left each other's company that evening very much connected. We knew we were right for each other. I slept like a baby with my sweats and high-tops still on, facedown on top of my covers. I slept knowing that if I could run four miles, I could do anything. I slept knowing that I had found the love of my life. I slept not wanting to move for fear that my legs would fall off, but I slept.

Turning the World Upside Down

Julie and I continued to spend time together daily. I knew she was the one for me. I had no doubt in the days and weeks to follow that we were going to spend the rest of our lives together. We were a match made in heaven and continue to be twenty years later. We took many walks (that's right, walks) down that road and continued to laugh about that night. We still laugh about it. We laugh at my tenacity to get a running date and her persistence in making me run the full four miles. We began to grow from each other's strengths and increased our effectiveness in reaching our goals as we worked together. We spent countless hours together walking, talking, studying and having fun.

Three months later in November, the autumn breezes signaled winter's subtle approach. Okay, it was not so subtle. After all, it was Wisconsin. We were spending virtually all of our free time together either by ourselves or with our friends. We were madly in love. One Sunday we decided to run some errands on the other side of town. Julie did not have a car at college, and I was in the middle of painting mine with my friend Jonathan Kurth. Truth be known, he was doing most of the work, but I made a good cheerleader. As a result, I asked David, the same David that I had told I would spend my life with Julie, if I could borrow his car. It was a two-year-old 1985 Ford Escort that his father had bought for him. David is a great guy and took great care of the car. I assured him that I would be careful with it, and I was.

Julie and I set out to complete our list of stops. We finished our first stop and were on our way to our second. Because they were only about three miles apart, I decided not to use my seatbelt. I always wore one, so this was unusual and out of character for me. I was being particularly careful and attentive because this was David's car, not mine. I was enjoying Julie's company and a day off with no classes and a little free time. The sky was overcast slightly as the afternoon wound down. It was 4:46 p.m. I recall looking down at the clock and seeing the digital readout. Because it was a Sunday, there was no rush-hour traffic.

As we drove south on Moorland Road just south of Interstate I-94 in Brookfield, I noticed that traffic in the right lane was slowing down. It is a three-lane road with a fourth lane being a turn lane. I looked into my left rearview mirror and over my left shoulder. I signaled and proceeded to switch lanes. As I drove into the center lane, I noticed how beautiful the sky looked as the gray overcast mixed with orange, red, and a hint of purple as the sun prepared to set. Julie and I were riding in new love and bliss.

Life can change in an instant...and it often does. Without any warning or hint of a catastrophe, we heard the indescribable and simultaneous sound of metal bending and glass and plastic shattering. Suddenly our car was in flight. We were to later learn that it had been hit with such speed and velocity that it flipped end to end twice and rolled three times. At the time, I just remember the world going by the outside windows in a blur of colors. There was also the continuous screeching sound of metal being twisted against its will and shrilling in an unsuccessful protest against being destroyed.

In an instant I saw Julie being thrown upside-down, sideways against the door, upright again, upside-down again. It was loud. The sights and the sounds were overwhelming. It was sensory overload and complete confusion. Then, all at once, it was silent. Julie was strapped in her seatbelt with shattered glass covering her.

She was saying, "I'm okay. I'm okay. I'm okay."

I was upside-down and managed to crawl sideways out through the door that had been involuntarily ripped open by the collision. The next few moments until the ambulance, police, and fire trucks came seemed like an eternity. I wanted to help Julie, so I crawled over to help her release the seatbelt that had no doubt saved her life. I felt excruciating pain in my back, as thought the muscles had been twisted and tied together and then pulled apart again by sheer force.

The emergency personnel came and asked us multiple questions. We could not think straight. We could not answer. We just kept watching each other to make sure that the other was all right. Apparently a custom conversion van was speeding and hit us with such velocity that we ended up upside-down facing the wrong way on the other side of the six-lane divided highway.

As we were taken to the hospital, they told Julie not to move or blink, or she could go blind. She was covered in glass. When you're told not to blink, the first thing that you want to do is to blink. But being the in-control and disciplined person that she is, she managed not to.

Once at the hospital, we were relieved to hear that Julie had sustained only minor cuts and bruises. She was banged up, but by the grace of God, nothing too serious. When they informed her of this, they also informed her about me.

"There is no easy way to tell you this, Miss," said the doctor, "but you are going to have to determine how much you care about your boyfriend and what that relationship means to you. You see, in the accident, his spine was injured severely. He has three breaks and, most likely, extensive nerve damage. I'm afraid that there is little chance that he will ever walk again."

"How bad are the breaks?" she asked.

"They are severe enough that we don't know the extent of the damage, but we can confirm that it is substantial. Patients with this type of injury rarely regain the use of their legs and often have other related effects. In his case, I would say that the chances are slim to none. I'm sorry, but that is where we are right now."

"I refuse to believe it," Julie responded.

"Miss, I can show you the X-rays. I can assure you that there are three breaks on the spine. You don't have to believe it, but the proof is there."

"That's not what I mean," she responded with certainty. "I believe that he has very serious injuries, but I refuse to believe that he won't walk again."

"The chances are so slim that I cannot offer you false hope."

"Hope isn't false. Hope gives determination and drive," Julie said with the confidence of someone who internally knows what is possible. "I know that this sounds crazy, but I know Chris, and if there is even the slightest chance that he can walk, he will. Not only that, but I know that all things are possible. God performs miracles and enables people to do things that others have said are impossible."

"That's a great attitude. I just hope that you're not disappointed."

"I won't be," said Julie.

The days that followed are somewhat blurred. The drugs that I was given made the world a haze. Julie recalls that I would fall asleep in the middle of a sentence. Although I am a fairly hyper person by nature, I am laid-back about taking things in stride. I get along with everyone and like to put the best construction on everything. At the same time, though, enough is enough.

My spirits were high (and so was I; wow, painkillers were my friends!), but you can only get stuck with a pin so many times. They used a pin to test whether I could feel my legs or feet. When I winced or screamed with pain, the doctor would say, "Good! That's very good!"

I was being stuck with a pin when I couldn't do anything about it, and what I wanted more than anything was to walk. Why? Because I wanted to get up, walk up to that doctor, give him a size 8D foot up his backside, and say, "Stop poking me with a pin, you little freak!" Unfortunately, that would have to wait as I could not yet walk.

In the days and weeks that followed, I was on fewer and fewer drugs, and they started elevating my torso in an attempt to fuse the spine together. It was about as comfortable as trying to find the light switch in the dark at a porcupine farm. I had no idea when the pain was going to come. It would just suddenly appear out of nowhere.

I could tell by the looks on their faces when the doctors and nurses started to get a spark of hope. They did not want to get too close to me with that spark, or I might explode. As an athlete, I was not used to being immobile. But in one day, I went from being the captain of a national cycling team to being told that I would never walk again. To say that I was going out of my mind in that hospital is as much of an understatement as saying that Richard Nixon could skew the truth from time-to-time. I wanted out, and I did not want to keep getting poked with a pin!

During this time, two people changed the course of my life and empowered me to design my destiny. Those people were Julie and one of my doctors. Julie never gave up hope, not even once. She was by my side daily. She would do her homework there. She would take notes there. She would make me laugh and crack jokes. Even more, she would tell me that I had to keep the vision of walking. She would tell me that I had to believe it, see it, feel it, and know that it would happen.

She would have me describe life when I was walking again. She would ask me to describe in detail what it felt like, both emotionally and physically, as if I were already doing it again. She would then ask me what had taken place to make that happen, as if we were looking back from the future. She would ask me what therapy I went through, as if the therapy had already happened and it was now a year later.

She would ask me what having less and less pain felt like, as if she was addressing me in a time when I no longer felt pain. Finally, she would ask me to describe the internal feelings that had caused me to go through the therapy and pain. What had pushed me? What had driven me?

She challenged me to find the same burning desire to walk again that had empowered me to run four miles without dying—or at least feeling like I was. She would even joke and say, "Hey, at least they have defibrillators here. There weren't any on our first and last run together. See, things are looking up already."

In short, she taught me to dig deep within and find a strength and determination that no one else could give to me. I had to find it myself. She was, and continues to be, my biggest and most significant inspiration in life.

The other individual who was instrumental was one of my doctors. He told me that many people with my types of injuries do not walk again, but that some do. He believed that those who did had an immovable conviction that they would. He shared books with me that described the mind-body connection—the power of the mind over the body and the ability of the body to do miraculous things. Everything that the experts had written supported what Julie was telling me constantly.

Together, Julie and I began to study more about the mind-body connection, the power of the mind and the healing power of the body. I became determined that I was going to own the goal of walking again. It would happen. I did not know how long it would take or what I would have to do, but I knew that I would walk again. I developed a conviction and a belief. My destiny did not reside in the unfortunate collision that had taken place. It did not reside in doctors, nurses, or even in Julie. My destiny resided in my ownership of my goals.

I could design my destiny. I realized this now. The more that I came to believe this, the faster and more fully my recovery began to take place. I began to realize that simply "desiring" my outcome was not enough. It was also not enough just to think about it or to talk about it. I had to believe it. Once I did, I had no doubt that it would happen.

I truly believe that I would not be walking today had God not blessed me with the ability to do so, and had Julie not shown me how to make the mind-body connection. I also believe that I would not have recovered as quickly if my doctor had not given me books to read and learn from. In the end, the biggest lesson that I learned is the power of God-given inner strength and conviction!

CHAPTER 4

LEAD BY EXAMPLE

THE BEST EXAMPLE YOU CAN SET IS PERSONAL SUCCESS

After days of the drugs wearing off and weeks of bed rest, therapy followed. It was painful but necessary. I will never forget when I was finally able to take my first steps without being held up by the nurses or therapists. All the thoughts and questions that Julie had presented to me came rushing back in an instant.

Having the ever-optimistic personality that I do and looking at life with a comedic outlook, I had visions of myself as Superman. I pictured myself standing there with my hands on my hips and a cape flying behind me...and realizing that those Superman tights could be very restricting. To the amazement of the doctors, nurses, and therapists, I was walking on my own. True, I looked like an imitation of Tim Conway's "old man shuffling" character from the *Carol Burnett Show*, but I was walking on my own. Slow speed is better than no speed when you have broken your back.

During my stay in the hospital, I noticed the different perspectives there. One was Julie's and my perspective, and the other was the medical personnel's. I was fighting to overcome what the medical professionals had told me was an insurmountable goal. They told me that the sooner I faced the reality that I would never be like I was before, the better off I would be. They explained that once I realized this, I could get on with my new way of life, limitations and all. I refused to believe this. Julie taught me to never give up, to keep pressing forward, and to believe in what could be possible. While I was doing this, I noticed the medical professionals doing just the opposite. Their self-imposed limitations were holding them back.

I would hear them say phrases such as, "I'm so tired, and I don't know how I am going to make it through this shift."

"I don't think we'll ever get this schedule right."

"It's impossible to get everything done that I need to during this shift."

"I can't get along with her because she is so unreasonable."

"This is going to be a difficult one."

I kept hearing all of these sentences voicing the thoughts that put limitations on them. Julie and I began to study what the medical personnel said and did, and to discuss why we thought they were like this. We reached the conclusion that they spent so much time caring for others that they did not make time to care for themselves. They had studied and found the power in medicine, but they needed to study themselves and find the power within. They were painting a picture of what was not possible, rather than what was.

The irony was that moving from one perspective to the other was like going from black to white. Julie and I would read about finding unlimited power within but see the hospital staff placing limits on what they thought they could do. The dichotomy seemed almost surreal. It was as if we were supposed to see the difference so that some day we could help others overcome whatever was holding them back.

This is really where the transformation began to take place. This is when we knew that we were to be leaders and trainers in the area of personal excellence. We became engulfed in our study of the power of the mind like fleas in a dog pound. There was so much to take in, learn, and experience. Everything went along normally between the staff and us during my struggle to regain the ability to walk. They waited for us to come to our senses, and Julie and I continued to strive. The breakthrough was the day that I actually walked on my own. That day changed everything between us and the staff.

They finally saw what could be possible, and they were amazed. They were amazed not just at my determination or Julie's continual support. They were amazed at what could be possible if a person finds the power within. They were changed by seeing the proof that came from belief. I suddenly became their pick-me-up pill each day.

I had never had so many nurses' visits in my life. One year earlier, I would not have minded because I did not know Julie then. In fact, a year earlier, when I was nineteen, I would have faked the injury for that much attention from females, much as any red-blooded college boy would do. Well, maybe I wouldn't have gone that far, but you get the point. They would come in the room smiling at Julie and me, literally humming or singing. They would smile and fluff my pillow or straighten my blanket. It was like the bearded lady at the freak show when I had to get up to use the restroom. They would all encourage me as I shuffled. One day they even clapped. Never, since I made "nice-nice" at two years old while learning to use the real potty, had anyone been so happy that I heard nature calling.

We learned that no matter what we shared with the staff verbally prior to my walking, they could not grasp the passion for themselves. They just did not get it. But once they saw the result of belief with their own eyes, they suddenly understood. Once they saw that miracles can and do exist in our lives, they began to get inspired. This experience brought home, in a way like never before, the phrases "Talk is cheap" and "Actions speak louder than words." We had been telling them all the great things we were reading and learning about the power within all of us, but life was just business as usual for them until they actually saw the end result.

After I started walking, nurses, doctors, X-ray technicians, receptionists, and other staff would come into the room one by one during different times of the day. They wanted to see the end result with their own eyes and to instill in themselves a new belief of what could be possible. Each time they came in, they would ask Julie or me a question about something that we had said to them before I began walking or something that they had heard someone else repeat after the walking began. There was a new and wonderful spark of hope and life in the staff of the hospital.

It was then that Julie and I realized that we had a mission and a purpose far greater than we had thought. We realized that if this staff was that much in disbelief, countless others must be living the same way. We believe that everything happens for a reason. We believed it before the accident, but it became much more personal when we saw how these injuries and this belief in recovery could affect so many people. We have had the humble privilege of being a living example for thousands of individuals for whom it has become crystal clear. We have seen others completely change their lives and their outcomes when they change their belief in what can be possible.

I missed much of the second semester of my junior year of college. Even though I was able to return to school some months later, I had to reduce the number of my classes. I also needed more sleep as my body recuperated and continued to get easily fatigued. As time went on, the fatigue and sleep began to return to normal, but the semester was still rolling.

It was a humbling and growing experience to ask for help when I needed it to function. I have always strived to be a gentleman. I like to open car doors, stand when a woman returns to the table at a restaurant, and let her go through a door first. I am very old-fashioned that way. Being this type of a person made it very difficult for me to have others, especially Julie, do the physical work for me.

When I returned to school, I was allowed to lift little to nothing at all. The doctors gradually increased the amount that I could lift, regulating the pressure on the back and preventing possible re-injury. Julie carried my tray in the cafeteria, my books to classes, and my laundry basket from the laundry room. She was amazing!

Through all this, I was learning a lot about myself and about life. I was learning what it meant to surrender control in an area of life. I was learning patience, something that I was told I didn't have before this. (I never slowed down long enough to listen, so I think this is what I'd been told. Who knows? I was in a hurry.) It was a healing time for me physically and a growing time for me as a person.

As the weeks went on, I gained a new appreciation for walking and moving. I gained a new appreciation for being able to walk Julie to her room and myself back to mine. Life itself seemed to have taken on a new perspective. I no longer looked at anything the same. Colors were brighter. Sounds were crisper. Breezes were more beautiful. Relationships were more precious.

I had not had a near-death experience as much as a potentially life-altering experience. For an active and athletic person, that meant changing virtually everything about my lifestyle. I could have done that if I had to. All of us have that power within ourselves, if we need to or choose to. But God, Julie, and my inner strength had given me a second option to choose, and I had chosen it. I felt empowered and freed by this. I was not, and still am not, the same person who shut the car door for Julie that day and walked around to the other side. I am not the same person who got in and turned the ignition for that fateful drive. And quite frankly, I am glad that I am not.

I had developed strength and determination that nothing could stop. I knew that if I could overcome a paralyzing injury when medical professionals said I could not, I could do anything. During my subsequent recovery, I played the role of "good boy" very well. I obeyed the rules and listened to the therapists. I increased my activity as allowed and cautiously began to increase the use of my back.

That summer, the summer of 1988, Julie and I chose to live on campus and work for Concordia University. It was perhaps even more of a transformational time for us than the previous months had been. A new door of learning had opened for us far beyond the world of traditional academic learning. We had become fascinated and almost obsessed with the power and possibility of human potential. Our reading list was much longer than anything assigned by our professors during the regular semesters. These were books that we had selected, tracked down, bought, or checked out of a library. We devoured them with the tenacity of a hungry hound off its leash at the corn-dog wagon at the state fair. Looking back, we must have looked comedic. We read until we fell asleep. We read over breakfast. We read walking to work on campus. We read while we were sorting mail for the university.

Julie and I had developed a quest for knowledge about human potential and a burning desire to revel not just in the miracle of my walking again, but in the fact that everyone has ability and potential that they most likely have not tapped. We looked back on the physical miracle that had taken place with me, but even more at the miracle that took place in the minds and lives of the hospital staff. When they began to believe what could be possible, they thought differently, talked differently, and interacted differently. Inspired by that, we must have read at least sixty books that summer. We were each reading about four books per week.

We began to study what "goal setting" really meant. Julie inspired me to have the goal of walking out of that hospital without any help. She taught me how to see it, believe it, and own it. It was up to me to live it. We did not study the topic of goal setting from any corporate manual. We did not even study goal setting under the topic of goal setting. We studied it as the topic of expected outcomes and designing your own destiny.

What we learned is that goal setting is usually associated with something that someone feels that they must or should do. This is the opposite of doing something because you want to. No one told me that I had to walk again and regain the full use of my legs. In fact, they had told me the opposite. Julie explained to me in that hospital room, in the midst of everything that was going on, that I had to want it badly enough to believe in it. She was right.

All summer, we continued to take notes, compare what we had read, discuss it, analyze it, and apply it to our lives. As we did, we learned more than we had in all our previous years combined. We joked that we were reading so much that summer that we would be tired of reading by the time the school year started again. Of course, we were completely wrong. We would get through our homework as fast as we could to get back to reading what we wanted to study more than anything else—human potential and the power of the mind.

The Beginning of our Journey

That fall I got engaged to the love of my life. On September 15, 1988 in the Te Deum Chapel at Concordia University Wisconsin, where we had our evening devotion time together, I asked Julie to marry me. Since I started our relationship on a lie and told her that I was a runner, I did not want to break tradition. As we sat in the second-to-last pew of the little chapel, I handed her a box. She asked what it was, and I told her that it was a gift…a set of earrings. As she opened the box, I asked her to marry me. Thankfully, she said yes.

Back in the hallway of our dorm, David Oberdieck learned of the engagement first. He got out a battery-operated bullhorn and announced it up and down the hallway. As he did, people began to emerge from dorm rooms, clapping and whistling. They came up to hug Julie and shake my hand or pat me on the back. A few offered Julie their condolences until David picked them up with the ease of a kindergarten teacher picking up a child. We knew that it was not only the beginning of our life together, but also the beginning of our journey to lead by example and empower others to live to their fullest potential.

That was my senior year of college. My original plans had been to take it easy and kick back, focusing more on work and earning money…and less on studying. Instead, I was scrambling to graduate on time since I had a double major and had missed a semester. I was taking twenty-one credits a semester, but I was completing them with greater ease than any other semester because I was focused. I knew that the faster I could complete my coursework, the sooner that we could get back to studying what we were passionate about. Julie and I both pulled straight As and were driven like never before. *When you understand goal setting from the inside out instead of the outside in, it is amazing what you can accomplish and how little effort it seems to take.*

The biggest lesson we learned was about giving vs. getting. We began to understand that there are two ways to look at life. The first focuses how much you can get for yourself. By nature, most of us tend to think this way. I still remember an episode of the TV show *MASH* in which Klinger asks Charles Emerson Winchester III for help. Charles' response was (insert Boston accent), "Klinger, let's look at this from a Winchester's point of view. What's in it for me?"

Isn't that how most people look at life? Isn't that how most of us approach projects, interactions, and relationships? We tend to take instead of give. It is a never-ending cycle that can lead to frustration and a constant reaching and grasping. Life can become like that of Wyle Coyote, ever in search of the illusive Road Runner.

Each time we think we have what we want, something else looks better. As a result, we are never quite satisfied or content. We spend an enormous amount of time and energy searching for something that always seems to elude us. It eludes us for one simple reason. It comes from the outside instead of the inside. "Getting" means taking something from outside, something that we do not have, and trying to use it to fulfill ourselves.

The other way that we can look at life is through the concept of giving. What can we give back? "Giving" implies that we already have something within that fulfills us. It implies that we have something worth giving. Something makes us so happy, so content, and so at peace that it fills every area of our life. As a result, we are so filled with joy that we want to share it with others. When this happens, we aren't focused on outcome but on purpose. Purpose is the reason for taking action. Living with purpose gives us a different outlook on everything. We begin to see what we have and feel blessed and privileged. We find joy in little things, in that which is, and what can be.

The Beginning of Your Journey

You may not have had a physical injury such as mine. Perhaps you had a different one. Perhaps you had an emotional injury from which you are still trying to recover. Maybe you have never had a serious physical or emotional injury at all. That is not the point, and neither is that fact that I had an injury. It isn't even whether you have had an injury of any kind. The point is that my injury and recovery started me on my own personal excellence journey. Julie was with me before, during, and after the injuries, which started her on her own personal excellence journey. For each of us, the journey begins in a different way at a different time.

Often people like to hear about individuals who were child prodigies or had business success early in life. We tend to like stories about the Mozarts of the world who began writing music at an early age. We want to hear about people like Bill Gates and Michael Dell who enjoyed monetary success early in life. But we need to expand our vision beyond that to see individuals like Colonel Sanders, who did not start his Kentucky Fried Chicken restaurants until he was in his sixties, and Mother Theresa, who did not begin her personal journey of excellence until she was in her forties. I invite you to focus on where you are right now—and where you want to be.

To help you to focus on the joy and fulfillment of giving vs. getting, I invite you to look at a related concept. As I mentioned when I spoke of our journey, there are two ways to look at life. We can look at life from the outside in or from the inside out. Most people tend to look at life from the outside in. They see what others have—where they live, what they drive, where they work, and how they live. They then compare themselves to others as if, for some unknown reason, this is the ideal that they must obtain.

Once they begin to study someone else's life, they begin to want a similar life themselves. After this, one of two things begins to happen. The first is that they may get what that other person has—the type of house, the model of car, or the professional position. However, when they do, they may find little to no satisfaction in that.

Why? Because they did not do it to own the goal but to mirror what they thought made someone else feel happy, successful, or completed. Whether the person they were mirroring actually felt happy, successful, or completed does not matter. The person doing the mirroring thought that was the case and, in essence, chased that other person's dream. As a result, attaining that dream did not give their lives meaning or bring them joy.

A second thing that may happen is a failure to reach that other person's situation or lifestyle. When this occurs, a person may feel as though he or she has failed and enter into a mind-set of disappointment and frustration. The goal was not happiness and contentment, but to be like someone else who was perceived to be happy and content. This is the type of thinking that we call living from the outside in.

Instead of thinking like this, I invite you to start your journey of personal excellence from the inside out. Begin first with you, not anyone else. Begin with where you are emotionally, physically, intellectually, and spiritually. Realize that you have within you the power to do and accomplish those things that will give your life joy and fulfillment. Realize that your happiness comes from within. You are completely in control of that.

When I took my first steps on my own in that hospital room, I felt great. If I was thinking from the outside in, I could have thought of how others in the hospital—whether they were staff, patients, or visitors—were walking faster and covering more ground than I was. I could have thought of those who were riding bikes or running (No, wait; running would bring back the gasping and panting). The point is that I had to start where I was. You need to do the same thing.

Don't be concerned with how someone else is doing; be interested and involved in how you are doing. Start by celebrating today! Start by celebrating you! Start by celebrating all that is possible and then take the first steps to make it happen. Don't worry about how someone else sees you. See yourself for how you really are and what you are really capable of.

If I had seen myself for how others saw me, I would not be walking today. Keep in mind that these were medical professionals talking about something about which they were experts. Still, they were not me. I didn't have to worry about what they thought was possible or impossible. I had only to develop my ability to believe.

Belief gives the ability to act, and action produces results. So begin by asking yourself what you feel that you are capable of having, being, and doing. While you are doing this, do not let other people put their limitations on you. If you do, you will be looking at what is in their glass instead of what is in yours.

Dare to Dream

As you begin your own journey, give yourself permission to dream. When you dream, dream big or dream small. Either way, don't place limits on yourself. Ask yourself, "If I could have, be, or do anything I wanted, what would that be?"

I have given you two examples from my life. The first was in dating Julie. The second was in recovering from an injury. In college, many young men wanted to date Julie. Some were taller than me. Some were better looking. Some had more money or nicer cars. Some were older than I was, and some were younger. None of that mattered to me. My focus was on Julie, not my so-called competition. As I lay on my bed with my sweats and high-tops still on after running those first four miles and hoping my legs did not fall off, I dreamed of spending my life with her. Even earlier, that dream pushed me to run those four excruciating miles, even while I had visions of running straight into the arms of a paramedic holding a defibrillator. I dared to dream. Because I dared to dream and then acted on that dream, my dream became a reality. We have been together for twenty years now.

Yes, about fifty other guys were perusing Julie, but they did not matter. Focusing on them would have taken mental and emotional energy away from my real goal—to date and fall in love with her. When you dream, do not focus on the things that could stand in the way of your dream. Do not focus on the things that could compete with you realizing your dream. Instead, focus on the dream itself. Focus on the outcome. Focus on giving all of yourself to the dream. In giving, we truly receive. We can achieve our dreams, whatever they are, if we unconditionally give of ourselves toward that end.

The second example that I gave was in walking again. But I want to take that a step farther. I did not just want to walk again; I wanted to ride again. I wanted to run (well…maybe not run), and play sports. I wanted to marry Julie and have children and push them on the swing and play tag and football with them. My point is to dream big.

Walking again was not a big enough dream. I had to look beyond that. I had to get a vision of what I really wanted in life. My immediate goal was to walk. My vision was a full recovery, which I was able to achieve over time because I believed with everything in me that my dream could, and would, come true. I did not want to walk simply to say, "I did it." It did not matter if anyone believed that I could, or even cared if I could. It mattered only to me. For me, it represented the first step to realizing a dream.

When I met Julie, just a few months earlier, I had developed and taken ownership of a dream. I dreamed of marrying her. I dreamed of making her happy and having children. I dreamed of a lifestyle of joy, laughter, playing, and celebrating life. You can do that if you are in a wheelchair and cannot walk. I am not saying that you can't. However, my dream for my life did not include that as part of the picture.

Dream big! If you simply create a dream for the immediate outcome and not the long-range happiness that you desire and deserve, you're selling yourself short. Ask yourself why you want that dream. Why is it important to you? What does it really represent? What larger need or want in your life will it fulfill? If you can begin to answer those questions, you will begin to powerfully and passionately pursue that dream at a new level.

What is your dream for your destiny? Whatever it is, it can start today if you do three things. First, believe in yourself and the power of you. Second, decide that you want your overall outcome badly enough that you will act. Third, take action! Whatever that action may be, big or small, take it!

I did not start by walking. I started by first being able to feel my toes. Then I wiggled my toes. Then I moved my legs. Then I moved with the assistance of a nurse. Then I moved with the help of a nurse while holding onto a walker. Finally, I walked on my own. It started small in my case.

Your first step towards designing your destiny and realizing your dream may be big or small. If you believe in your ultimate outcome and you decide to take action, whatever size that step is, it is a huge one for you! Your new and exciting future can begin now if you simply make the decision to take action. Remember, you are in control of your destiny!

Chapter 5

Superglue Your Crystal Ball

What You Look For You Will Find

In 1993 Julie and I were living in Oklahoma. I was working on my doctorate in psychotherapy and driving regularly between Tulsa and Oklahoma City. I really enjoyed the people there. They are honest, open, neighborly, and sincere. I enjoyed my time with them and socialized a lot. As a result, I thought that I fully understood the people of Oklahoma and what they may do differently than us from the Midwest. I could not have been more wrong on one particular day.

It was a Sunday, and after church we were going to drive to Miami, Oklahoma (pronounced My-am-a). It was a beautiful, typically hot and dry Oklahoma day with the temperature in the mid-nineties. As we were driving, we came to the outskirts of Pryor Creek (pronounced Pryor Crick). Pryor Creek is a small town not much larger than Shaquille O'Neal's high-tops. In fact, when you pulled out of your driveway there, you could say you were on the outskirts, no matter where your driveway was. The land is flat and open, so in many places, you can see for miles. We were driving towards Stillwater when Julie pointed out a large pillar of smoke "just down the road a spell," as they say in Oklahoma.

"Wow, something sure is on fire," Julie said in amazement. The thick smoke went straight up and curved ever so slightly to the left.

"Gee, I hope everyone is okay," she said with concern.

"Me, too," I agreed.

"Do you know how to get to Harold's place from here?" she asked.

"I think so, but I'm not sure."

"Perhaps we should stop for directions."

I readily agreed. That is the thing about having five sisters and multiple nieces. You learn to ask for directions. I have three brothers, too. However, they are "typical" males, with that sense of direction gene, and never have to ask for directions. Somehow I missed the gene and can get lost on my way to the mailbox at the end of the driveway if I am not paying attention. I often wonder: If I get Alzheimer's forty years from now, will I actually know where I am going for once?

We pulled into the local gas station. Let me rephrase that. Everything is local in a town the size of Shaquille O'Neal's high-tops. So, let's just say we pulled into the gas station.

"Howdy!" said the attendant whose shirt proudly displayed the name "Ray."

"Hi, Ray," I said. "How are you today?"

"I'm better than a turkey with a turbo at Thanksgiving time," he said, pushing back a cap that displayed the words "Snap-on Tools."

"I reckon you're lost or somethin', huh?"

"Not really, Ray, but we're trying not to be."

"I sees where you're comin' from," he said with a smile. "Don't wanna end up like the only cow in the bullpen during mating season, huh?"

I am a city boy by nature. That was more information than I needed. I quickly responded before I got any uninvited visuals based on his reference.

"Here's where we're headed," I said as I showed him the address.

"Uh huh," he said to himself and mentally digested the information from the map. "Uh huh.....huh.....emhmm.....yup."

I didn't want to interrupt his flow of genius.

"Okay, here's what you want to do," he said, putting his arm on my shoulder and pointing up the road.

"Go up the road a spell, maybe a mile or so. Find the dirt road by the little rock. Not the big rock. You do not want that one; that'll take ya clear in the opposite direction yer wantin' to go. Take the dirt road by the little rock."

That's it, I thought to myself. *We will never be heard from again. It's over. I can see the headlines now: "Lost in Oklahoma, Somewhere Past the Big Rock—Not the Little Rock."*

"Once you're on that road, stay on it for five, maybe six miles. It will fork by the big set of trees."

Five "or" six miles? You can get really lost really fast in one mile in the middle of nowhere Oklahoma, I thought to myself.

"When you get to the big set of trees on your left, turn to your right. The road is hard to see, but you'll find it."

Sure, I thought to myself. *Find it like a single-engine aircraft that went down "somewhere" in the middle of the Pacific.*

"Once you've turned right, watch out for the ostriches."

"Ostriches?" I said out loud in surprise and disbelief.

"Yeah, you know, ostriches," he said and started walking around me with his knees up high, his thumbs tucked under his armpits, and his head bobbing forward and back. "Ostriches, the other white meat. Watch out fer 'em. They can get reeeal mean this time of year," he said as he leaned his face about six inches from mine and said "SQUACK!" so loudly that I jumped.

"Don't mind 'em though. Just slow down enough to not startle 'em, and you'll be fine," he continued. "Don't stop or they'll feel threatened. Don't speed up, or they'll get confused and run in front of your car. Don't try to get their attention. And don't, I repeat, don't make eye contact with 'em. They'll take that as a challenge. Just slow down a scooch and just keep makin' yer way through, and you'll be fine. Once you make your way past the ostriches take a left at the first thicket of trees. Take that four miles and shazaam! You're in Stillwater."

"Shazaam!" I said in comedic agreement.

"Shazaam!" he said more emphatically as he slapped me on

the back. At least he wasn't being the human ostrich at the moment.

"Thanks, Ray," I said.

"No problem. Need any gas?"

"No thanks, but thanks for asking."

"Any oil?"

"No thanks, but thanks for asking."

"Pop?"

"We're good."

"Snacks?"

"Really, Ray, we're good."

I was starting to feel like Steve Martin's character, Neal Page, from the movie *Planes, Trains, and Automobiles* when John Candy's character, Del Griffith, kept offering to buy him something at the airport to make up for stealing his cab. Only in this case, Ray was simply trying to be nice.

"Suit yourself," he said with a smile. "You need anything; y'all just come on back now, ya hear."

"Thanks, Ray. See ya."

I got to the car, and Julie said, "Why was he walking like a chicken?"

"He wasn't." I said through laughter. "It was an ostrich. I'll explain as we drive."

"Could you get me something to drink, please?" she asked. "It's really hot and I'm really thirsty."

Oh boy. I just turned down multiple offers, yet here I go again.

As I got out of the car, Ray commented, "That was quicker than a toad in a tornado."

More visuals.

"Whatcha need?" he asked.

"Just a cold drink for Julie."

"Regular or diet?"

"Uh? Diet. Diet would be fine."

"Bottle or can?"

"Either is fine."

"Got 'em both. What's your preference?"

"Uh, can. A can is fine."

"Glass or no glass with that?"

"No glass is fine."

"Straw?"

"Sure."

"Okeedokee. Comin' right up!"

I felt like I just made his day. He came out whistling and wiping the can off with a hand towel. He meant well, but I got the feeling it was cleaner before the towel.

"Here ya go. It's on the house."

"Are you sure?" I asked.

"As sure as a house cat knows how to stay away from the coyotes." As I got back into the car, he said, "'Member now, y'all watch out for the ostriches!" while raising his knees, sticking his thumbs under his armpits, and bobbing his head.

"Will do," I said, trying not to laugh.

As we drove up the road, Julie looked in the rearview mirror from the driver's seat and burst into laughter. We were at least a quarter mile away from the "fillin' station," as he called it.

"Look out the back window," she said laughing.

As I turned to look, I saw Ray standing at the end of the station parking lot, still waving good-bye and doing the ostrich dance. Believe it or not, there are some things about Oklahoma that I will always treasure as wonderful. "Fillin' Station Ray" is one of them.

The "Pink Boeing"

As we were driving, Julie pointed out that the smoke we had seen earlier had increased in thickness and size.

"Julie," I said, suddenly realizing where it was coming from. "That's coming from Ken's farm!"

"Holy cow, you're right!" she agreed. "I hope everything is all right!"

"Maybe we should drive over there and find out."

"Great idea," she agreed. "He and Sally are getting up there in years. We don't want to take any chances."

Ken and Sally went to church with us. They were wonderful, salt-of-the-earth people. When we moved to town and I began studying for my doctorate, we met them at church. Julie and I had no children at the time and were living in a small town, so we felt that one car was all that we needed. That would save us insurance, gas, and upkeep, and we could save our money while I went to school and worked. When Ken realized that we had only one car, he had taken it upon himself, without asking, to trade a bunch of scrap sheet-metal to another farmer for a car. He wanted to do something special for the "nice young couple at church," as he and Sally referred to us.

As we drove towards the pillar of smoke, I recalled a specific day that we had visited Ken and Sally's place a few months earlier. That day he had invited us over for lunch. While we were there, he said, "Come on outside, Chris. I've got a surprise for you."

"You do?" I asked genuinely surprised.

"Yup," he said chuckling to himself and shaking his head from side to side while looking down as if he had pulled off something of huge importance.

We walked outside and into his barn. As we walked, he was all grins and giggles. He was a wonderful what-you-see-is-what-you-get kind of man. He wore old, worn-out Western shirts with snaps on the sleeves. Because the sleeves were too short for Ken's big frame, they always hung unsnapped and open. His pants were always either black or brown, usually with a hint of barbeque sauce or pork-rind crumbs on them. His cowboy boots most likely pre-dated me and had been resoled more times than Elizabeth Taylor has been married.

"There she is," he said with his arm around my shoulder.

He pulled two unwrapped pieces of beef jerky from his pocket.

"Jerky?" he offered.

"Thanks, but no thanks."

"Suit yer'self," he said, smiling and taking a big bite while keeping his arm around my shoulder.

"It's all yours! What do ya think?"

"For me?" I asked, hoping that I had misheard him as my face turned paler than Michael Jackson's.

"Yup! For you and the lil' missus," he said, prouder than a father whose son had just won a tournament on the PGA tour.

"Oh, Ken," I said. "You shouldn't have." I meant it. He really, really shouldn't have.

There in front of me was a 1978 Ford Fiesta four-speed. It has once been red but was now Oklahoma sun-faded, Pink-Panther pink. It had a black interior sun-faded to light gray with cracks on every conceivable part of the vinyl surface. The steering wheel was wrapped with a very old, very dry-rotted steering-wheel cover that was not cool even in 1978 when some retired fellow put it on there to preserve his investment. The steering-wheel cover had once been dark blue, but the top had faded to a powder blue, giving the cover a natural tie-dyed look.

The two front rims were smaller than the back ones. The car looked like a bad attempt at a hotrod conversion because its back was raised slightly due to the oversized rims. The antenna was broken off exactly halfway down and bent awkwardly forward like a flying saucer model from a 1956 black-and-white science fiction film.

As we walked around the side of the car, I said, "You really...really shouldn't have."

He was smiling and beaming like a Sunday school boy with a new suit and an ice cream cone.

I wasn't kidding. He really shouldn't have.

"I couldn't possibly accept this," I said looking for a way out of the "Pink-Mobile."

"You have to," he assured me. "I can't get my scrap metal back, and I don't fit in it," he said rubbing and patting a belly that looked as if he were due any day.

"What about Sally?" I asked in desperation. "She would love this car."

"Nopers," he said, while looking down and shaking his head with his eyes closed.

Looking up, he pointed inside the window as he put his arm around my shoulder and leaned me forward. "She don't know how to drive stick or nothin'."

I looked inside. It was a manual transmission. On top of the stick shift was a round circle that said "8" like a pool ball.

It got worse. Somewhere along the line, someone had added a gas pedal cover shaped like a giant, chrome bare foot. I could just hear them singing "Feeling Groovy" as they installed it.

I was not feeling groovy.

The gas pedal rested on a floor mat that was faded black with white daisy-like flowers. The flowers had faded Big Bird yellow with age.

"Had 'em throw in the floor mats for the lil' missus. I thought Julie might like a 'feminine touch' in case she ever drove it," he said, nudging me in the side with his elbow.

"You really…really shouldn't have," I once again affirmed.

"You have to take it, or I'll be offended," he said with fatherly sternness.

He meant it.

I looked toward the back. The tailpipe was firmly fastened to a hole that had been drilled into the body. A fresh, newly fastened coat hanger gripped it firmly. Ken reached down and slapped the tailpipe.

"She ain't goin' nowheres," he said chuckling. "I done fixed her real tight for ya."

"Wow (pregnant pause)…thanks, Ken."

I was dumbfounded. I did not know what to say.

"Best part about it is that everything works but the radio and the air conditioning." He chuckled and put his arm around me as together we bent over to look at the radio. "The eight-track works just fine, though," he proudly announced.

Oh, that's okay, Ken," I assured him, "I don't own any eight-tracks."

He started to chuckle again.

Uh oh.

"I gotcha covered there, too, lil' buddy," he proclaimed walking away. He went behind the barn door and reappeared with a cardboard box. "I thought you might not have any, so I scrounged up some good ones at the flea market the other day when I was in town." He handed me the box. "Shoot. They had some good ones that day. I lucked out!" he said.

I looked down and saw a variety of eight-track tapes. Freddy Fender, Slim Pickens, Charlie Pride, The Bee Gees, Earth Wind and Fire, Abba, and two Barry Manilow tapes.

"Wow...thanks."

"Don't mention it," he said, patting me on the back.

This could not get any better. Pryor Creek, Oklahoma gets in the nineties…then it gets hot. I was now the proud owner of a non-air-conditioned Pink Mobile with vinyl seats. To top it off, I sweat like a pig (which is ironic because technically pigs do not sweat that I know of, but I digress). I was getting visuals of looking like the sweating airline pilot from the original movie *Airplane.*

He handed me the key and said, "Don't lose it. I only have one. Go ahead. Fire her up!"

"Now," he explained, "you have to pump it ten, maybe twelve times, and she should fire right up."

Pump, pump, pump, pump, pump, pump, pump, pump, pump, pump, pump, pump. I kept pumping the oversized, chrome barefoot gas petal. I turned the key.

BANG! It backfired. I jumped.

"That's all right. Try her again," he said without hesitation.

I turned the key, and it started. Suddenly this tiny little pink car was making a sound like a Boeing 747 taxiing down the runway at O'Hare Airport.

RUUUUUUUMBLE!

"Oh yeah," he said, screaming to overcome the humungous noise the car was making. "There is a hole in the exhaust 'bout this big," he said putting his hands in the shape of an "O" and looking at me through it.

Great, I thought. *Now I can't "sneak" into town in the Pink Mobile. I will be formally announced.*

As he was standing there, I began to lose sight of him through the vast, thick cloud of blue smoke engulfing the Pink Mobile. It was almost the same shade as the faded seats but with a bluer hue.

"That's a good sign!" he said, giving me two thumbs up.

"It is?" I asked in shocked disbelief.

"Yuppers," he assured me.

"When I first saw it, I was concerned," he said. "Then I realized it's blue, not white."

I see, I though to myself. *How color-sensitive of you.*

He reached in and shut it off. "Come with me," he said as he walked to the front of the car.

For a brief moment, he was still screaming until he realized that the noise competition had ceased.

"Let's pop the hood and I'll show you."

I reached back in to find the hood-release latch.

"No need," he said. "That broke. No worries. I jury rigged it." He adjusted yet another coat hanger, and the hood popped open. It was not the other half of the coat hanger on the back. I knew this for two reasons. First, he used an entire coat hanger on the back. Second, the one on the back was bright, bright yellow and this one was dark green. He opened the hood and propped it up with a makeshift hood prop, a yardstick.

"Keep this away from the engine," he said in a teaching voice while holding up the yardstick. "It's combustible. Keep it over here and it'll be fine," he said and pointed to the side of the wheel well. *How this man has stayed alive for sixty-eight years is beyond me*, I thought to myself in amazement.

"See, here's why the blue smoke is good news," he said,

pointing to the engine. "If it was white, it would mean you have a cracked block and antifreeze got mixed in. Blue means it's just oil."

"I see," I said.

"You're okay, though," he said pointing down into the engine compartment next to the battery. "Just keep this with you, and add a bit every couple of days," he said lifting the quart of motor oil that was resting between the battery and the fender inside the engine compartment.

Great! That's two combustible things to keep away from the engine. The good news is that everyone that I grew up with or have worked with lives somewhere other than Oklahoma. No one needs to know about this, I thought to myself.

He shut the hood, and we walked back to the house.

Walking in, he looked at Sally and Julie. "You shoulda' seen the look on his face," he said, as he hugged me with his left arm and nearly crushed my bones. Ken was about six-foot-one but slouched over so he was only about two inches taller than I am.

After lunch that day, Julie and I drove home. Actually, Julie drove home and told me to give her a good head start so that she would not be associated with the Pink Mobile. As we drove home, it was evident to all that I was arriving. As I accelerated, birds, small animals, and children ran for cover at the sound of the "Pink Boeing." When I stopped, the car would die and a large thick cloud of blue smoke would come from the back and envelope the exterior and the interior.

As if that did not get enough attention, it stalled at about every other intersection. After I pumped the chrome foot-pedal several times, the car would start with a loud "BANG!" like some make-believe car from an early '70s Disney movie. At one point I could not get it started, so I tapped my horn to try to get Julie's attention to wait for me. Tapping the horn was a mistake.

It stuck on!

Consider the whole effect. Once started, the Pink Boeing emerges slowly from a thick blue cloud like a David Copperfield magic show. It is faded pink with oversized rear rims and louder than a jet—with a horn that won't shut off.

"Yes. That's right. I am studying for my doctorate," I said to my imaginary crowd. "Don't I look sophisticated?"

Eventually the horn stopped. But it was really hot. It was in the mid-nineties and humid, which is rare in Oklahoma unless it is about to rain. Luckily, or unluckily, the Pink Boeing had a sunroof with a crank handle. I was sweating like a cowboy on a bull before the chute opens. I was desperate, so I opened the sunroof all the way. As fate would have it, the humidity turned to a downpour no more than three minutes later.

Well, at least I got a breeze for a few moments, I assured myself.

As I went to shut the sunroof, the handle broke off. The sunroof was now stuck open, and it was pouring—I looked pathetic.

At the next stoplight, I pulled up next to a family who looked at me with such disbelief that they must have been thinking, *When did they let him out?* I was in the Pink Boeing with the yellow coat hanger holding up the muffler. It was making more noise than a Boeing 747, and I was slowly disappearing into a blue cloud while rain drenched both me and the interior.

That was the last time I drove that car. I didn't want to hurt Ken's feelings, though, or damage our relationship—I thought of a plan. Every couple of days, I put it in neutral, moved it forward or back in the driveway, and turned the front wheels to make it look as though it had been driven. When we moved to Chicago the following year, we sold the car in Pryor Creek, saying that we just could not get it back home. Ken offered to bring it up on his trailer. Shaking his hand with my other hand on his shoulder, I assured him that he had already done quite enough.

Where's the Fire?

This entire car episode was going through my mind as we approached where Ken and Sally lived. They were kind, and we liked them a lot. Sure, we like to make fun of the gift they gave us, but they opened their hearts to include us in a way not many people can. We were a part of their family, if even for a short time. This was important to two people who were "not from around these parts." We were raised to feel more comfortable with more buildings and fewer animals, but graduate school had taken us out of our comfort zone for a short time. It was good for us to expand our horizons, and it was a blessing to find such loving people.

As we pulled up, I began to get concerned. "Lord only knows what he could have done," I said to Julie.

"I hate to guess," she replied with a wide-eyed look.

As we pulled up to his farm, we were both shocked. His field was on fire!

"Holy smokes," I exclaimed. "Ken's field is on fire!"

My heart sank.

"Oh, my gosh!" Julie gasped.

She sped up as we approached their farm. It was a hot, dry Oklahoma day, and it would not take long for the fire to spread. Julie pulled into the driveway and slowed down, and I opened the door before she had even stopped. I jumped out, leaving the door open, and sprinted toward the large hose that lay by the barn. I grabbed it and ran to the faucet (or "spicket" as they liked to call it). I opened it all the way.

As I ran toward the fire with the hose, I wondered, where in the world could Ken and Sally be? I wondered if their house was open to call the fire department. Keep in mind that this was 1993. I did not get my first cell phone until later that year.

I began to spray the fire. It must not have started much earlier because I was able to start putting it out. Another few minutes, and it would have been much bigger.

As I continued to extinguish the fire, Ken came out of the house.

"What are you doing?" he asked in a loud, quite surprised and concerned voice.

"Ken, you're home!" I said in amazement. *How could he have not known about the fire?*

"'Course I'm home," he said matter-of-factly as he began to walk toward the "spicket."

"Where else would I be when I'm burnin' my field?" he said, as if I made no sense whatsoever.

"Burning your field?" I asked.

He walked over and started to turn the water off.

"We don't add water for another ten minutes."

I don't get it, I thought to myself. *He's not the type to commit insurance fraud, and I don't think he's lost his mind in the twenty-four hours since I saw him last.*

He walked over, took the trickling hose out of my hands, and pointed to the field with a smile. "Good thing I got here when I did. Another few minutes, and you would have watered my field down too much to burn. I've been waitin' for a hot, dry day like today."

"I just don't get it," I said, genuinely confused.

He pointed to the field and smiled again.

"I'm burning my fleas."

"Burning...your...fleas?"

"See, you're not from around here," he said in a friendly father-like tone. "'Round these parts, when it gets hot, fleas get out of control. Only thing you can really do is burn 'em."

"What about your field?"

"It grows right back."

"It does?"

"Suuure," he said, while starting to sprinkle the fire that was rapidly volleying with him like a good tennis match. "Look at a forest fire. The forest grows back faster and thicker than before," he said with the certainty of a museum guide. "Same thing here, only when it grows back, I have fewer fleas to worry about."

I talked with him for a while as he kept the fire under control, carefully letting it spread, extinguishing it a bit, and then letting it spread again. He did this over and over again. He seemed to know what he was doing. He had obviously done this for many years, and it obviously worked for him.

Lessons in Leadership

Looking back, I realize now that I learned many lessons about life and leadership from living in Oklahoma. Julie and I like to joke about living there because it was so different from what we had experienced at the time. However, living there changed and shaped us in a wonderful way. It expanded our horizons, and it was a significant part of our study of personal excellence and high-performance leadership. Let me share a few of the lessons that we learned from living in Oklahoma. As you read them, maybe you can apply them to your own journey as well.

Lesson One: Take time to notice the Filling Station Rays. Whether you live in California, New York, Minnesota, Texas, or anywhere in between, you'll have Filling Station Rays. They may not talk like Oklahoma Ray. Hopefully, they do not walk like an ostrich, but if they do, take the time to appreciate life and laugh with them. These are people you encounter every day who are honest, open and caring. They can lead you in directions that you want to go but don't know how to get to. Often, they can help you avoid pitfalls or mistakes that you otherwise would have rushed into.

For example, after we had driven to the fire at Ken's farm, we continued on our way with the directions that Ray had given us. Before leaving, however, I doubled-checked the directions with Ken, since we were at his house anyway.

Reading over the list while watering his fire, he mumbled the directions under his breath as his mind's eye drove the route. "Little rock, big rock, right, trees, two miles..." then he trailed off. Looking back at the fire, he said, "Yup, perfect directions all right." As we were leaving, he said, "Watch out for the ostriches, though. They are really 'awnry' this time of year."

He confirmed it, just as Ray had said.

Keep an eye open for the Filling Station Rays in your life. They may be funny or goofy, but they can give you good information. Remember, leaders are listeners and can take input and directions from many different reliable sources. Just because someone is quiet or unassuming, do not write that person off. Many times they are the eyes and ears that we may fail to be in our fast-paced lives with endless to-do lists. Ask their input, listen to their directions, and then add your own judgment.

By the way, Ray was right. Right where he said there would be ostriches, there they were. They looked like they were just wandering around, but when our car approached, they started to squawk and get upset. Julie slowed down, and they stopped squawking and watched us drive through. It was just as Ray had said.

Lesson Two: Be grateful for the Pink Boeings. They show you are loved. I did not want a faded red-to-pink 1978 Ford Fiesta with no air-conditioning and cracked vinyl seats. Ken, however, had traded his scrap metal for the car because he cared. The car was old and worn out. That was not the point. The point was the thought behind the gesture. Yes, it was a long and comedic ride home. It was embarrassing to say the least, but it only lasted a short time. Okay, so at the time it seemed like an eternity, but looking back now, I can laugh. However, the love that Ken offered is still felt today.

You will get Pink Boeings in life. Look past them, and see the vulnerable human beings who were open enough to give them to you. Remember that the Pink Boeing means that you are loved. It means someone cares for you. It truly is the thought behind the gift that counts. Be genuinely thankful for the emotion behind the gift.

If you have children, you know exactly what I mean. They give you things and do things for you with honest intention. When they are young, they may pick out a piece of clothing for you that you would not choose in a thousand years. They may have even used their own piggybank money. They may make you a sandwich that is barely edible, but they make it with love and with their own two little hands.

So what do you do? You wear the plaid pants and make sure that you tell everyone that your son or your daughter picked them out just for you. Their skepticism at your fashion sense will turn to a heartwarming smile, especially if they have been in your place. And you eat the sandwich. You wash it down with a smile because, although you would not make it, it is made with love.

Adults are just kids in bigger bodies. When the Kens and Sallys of this world get you a Pink Boeing, remember their feelings. Use earplugs for the exhaust if you need to, hold your breath through the blue smoke (hey, at least it is not white), smile, and say a *sincere* thank you. True leaders appreciate the thought behind the effort. Just don't open the sunroof if it is raining.

Lesson Three: Don't act until you know the desired outcome. Ken had waited long and hard for just the right day when his field would be ready to burn. I meant well, but I almost ruined his outcome. I cared about Ken, so I leaped into helping mode. The reality is that he did not ask for help because he did not want or need the help. He knew what he was doing. Even though I thought this was an emergency, it was not. Even though I thought that he was being careless, he was not. Even though I thought I should rush in without asking, I should not have.

More than that, I did not just help; I took over. In my imaginary Superman suit, I ran into action. (And let me tell you, those tights can be very uncomfortable on a hot Oklahoma day.) I was not doing it for an ego boost. I was doing it for all the right reasons. Unfortunately, even though the reasons were right, the action was not helping. I learned much from that.

Just recently, Julie was busy with a big project for the family. She and the kids are my life, and my world literally revolves around them. I can truly say that I am the most blessed man in the world to have them in my life. Normally, Julie cooks dinner while I try to get home on time, or if we can pull it off, we cook together. This particular day, I called proudly announcing that I had pushed hard on some important work-related projects and was arriving home in time for dinner.

There was silence on the other end of the phone. This was followed by, "Oh my, I was so involved in my project that I didn't notice the time. I haven't even started dinner."

I wait for these opportunities. She does so much for the kids and me. She gives more of herself than I can fathom. This was my chance to show her how much I love her and how grateful I am for her.

"Don't worry, honey, I will cook for you. Relax. I love you."

On the other end of the phone, I instantly heard all the tension melt away. She was truly grateful. Now, before you think that I am tooting my own horn or playing Super-Husband, keep reading.

I arrived home, and changed out of my suit and into my play clothes. That may sound funny to you, but moms are moms. They make their kids change out of their church or school clothes so they will not mess them up, and they make their husbands change out of their suits. Julie may be 5'3", but I don't have the guts or the gumption to say no when she tells me to change.

As I entered the kitchen, our son asked, "Whatcha doin'?"

"Making dinner so that Mommy does not have to."

"Can I help?" he asked with nine-year-old eyes the size of bowling balls. He loves doing anything for his mommy, as does our daughter. On this day, it happened to be Connor. On any given day, it could be Connor or Kelsey.

Snapping into task mode as I looked at the clock, and with total disregard for his feelings, I said, "No."

"Oh...okay," he said obediently and walked out of the room with a feeling of being neither wanted nor appreciated.

I felt as thought I'd been sucker-punched in the stomach. I did. I physically felt ill, and I had done it to myself. My world revolves around Julie and the kids. I had just upset the balance of my life, and I felt the pain and shame that I deserved.

"Sure you can help, Tiger!" I said.

"Really?" he said, instantly right beside me as if he had been teleported from the other room like on the original *Star Trek.*

With each new item that was needed and with each new food that I cooked, the question was the same, "Can I help?"

What beautiful words. I was twenty-six when I rushed to Ken's field without asking. I had just assumed. Connor was nine and asked if he could help. He never assumed. We can learn a lot from children.

It took longer to cook together. It was much messier to cook together. However, it was beautiful. That leads to the final lesson I wish to share with you in this chapter.

Lesson Four: Take the time to learn from children because they have much to teach you. Whether you do or don't have children or grandchildren of your own, learn from children. Learn from yours or someone else's. The point is, just learn from them. Our children are eight and ten as we write this book. Just a couple of years ago, they began to ask, over and over again, when we cooked, "Can I help?" More and more, my answer is "Yes." I am learning the importance not just of them experiencing the actions, but of me experiencing *them.*

That day Connor helped me cook, I learned much about his patience, his quiet persistence, his affection, his love for his mommy and his family, and his desire to be included. Look around you. Who can you include in your life and learn from? Ask yourself that question, and you will be glad that you did.

We each have a crystal ball. It's our vision of our life and our future. Unfortunately, we sometimes look so hard at what we don't have that we fail to see what we do have. When we look at what we don't have or where we perceive we should be in life, it is as if we have dropped our crystal ball. The ball becomes chipped or, worse yet, it shatters.

When that happens, pick up your crystal ball and super-glue it together again. Then, if you look hard enough into your crystal ball, you will see what you have in your life right now. You will see how beautiful and good life is. You will see people all around you who care about you. You will see people around you from whom you can joyfully learn and grow. You will see a present life of good things and a future with unlimited possibility!

Remember, what you look for, you will find. What you find, you will attract. What you attract, you will become. That is your destiny! So, pick up that crystal ball, super-glue it back together, and start seeing the good in your life now that will lay the groundwork for an amazing future.

Chapter 6

It's Raining Tomatoes

It's Not What You See, But How You See It

Most of us want to get to the point in life where we hear a voice from the clouds saying, "The fasten-seatbelt light is turned off; you can now move about your life freely." On an airplane, we are told to keep our seatbelts fastened when the plane takes off, lands, or experiences turbulence. This keeps us from bouncing around like Tigger from *Winnie the Pooh and Friends.* Having the seatbelt on during calm times is recommended so that we are still secure if a sudden disruption occurs. It is optional because the light is only turned off when the pilot expects smooth flying.

Most of us want to get to the point of smooth flying in our lives. We want to have a strong enough handle on personal excellence so that our actions and interactions with others are smooth, enjoyable, and productive. While we can't avoid turbulence in our lives and relationships, effective leaders have learned to keep their emotional seatbelts fastened to handle the unexpected. How do they do this? How can you begin to move in this direction for more effective interactions and positive outcomes during turbulence? The answer can be found by looking at the life of the late Floyd Haskens.

"Who was Floyd Haskens?" you ask.

He lived in Norman, Oklahoma, and passed away in the 1990s. We had the good fortune to meet and get to know Floyd in 1991 while we were living in Norman during our first year of marriage. Floyd had one speed—medium. He was never super-slow and never in a hurry. At first glance, Floyd seemed to be a penniless bachelor. That is what most people thought until the day that he died. Those of us who came to know and love him for who he was, knew that this initial impression was wrong. In fact, nothing could have been farther from the truth.

When Julie and I met Floyd, he was in his early 70s. He was a lifelong bachelor who looked like he was waiting for his next Social Security check to buy groceries. He wore overalls seven days a week, rain or shine, warm or cold. He exchanged them for a suit on Sunday mornings for church, for special occasions, or for monthly senior-group Bible studies at church. Even then, the two similar suits that he owned clearly were out-of-date by society's standards, but not by Floyd's.

"Nice suit, Floyd," I said to him at the monthly senior Bible-study lunch that I was leading. I meant it, too. He kept it nice and, although out of date, it looked good on Floyd.

"You like it, Chris?" he said with a boyish smile.

"I really do," I affirmed as I looked into his eyes, which were the same blue as a robin's eggs. He set down his plate of food and slowly, steadily arranged each piece of silverware an equal distance from the plate and from each other. Floyd paid attention to details and took his time doing so. His hair, white and as fine as a baby's, was parted perfectly to the side. Like a ten-year-old boy, he had combed it in the morning, and now it was flopping on his forehead. At the back was a huge cowlick that any mother would send her son back to the mirror to fix.

As he leaned forward, his bangs slid down his forehead and almost covered his eyebrows. Floyd did not see the need to waste money on frequent haircuts because he always wore a John Deere baseball hat with his overalls. He would get his hair cut really short and then go longer without haircuts to save money.

Brushing his bangs back with his weathered fingers, he sat down and smiled. When he smiled, his face looked like the Bonneville Salt Flats with hundreds of lines showing that he had spent a lifetime in the sun, and that he had smiled often. He extended his arm, turning it upside down and then right side up again as he admired his suit.

He elbowed me and said, "When I bought this suit back in 1973, they didn't know what they were doing."

"How's that?" I asked with genuine curiosity.

"I bought this black one, and they gave me a second one for

free," he giggled. "I didn't want to look like I was wearing the same suit all the time," he continued, "so I got the other one in brown. It doesn't surprise me that they went out of business, giving away their merchandise like that."

"You got a great deal and a lot of mileage out of those if you have had 'em since 1973," I assured him.

Laughing in a gentle and boyish manner, he replied, "If this suit was a car, it would still be low mileage. It's old, I know, but I hardly ever wear it. Most folks probably laugh and think it's out of date and that I look funny. My mama used to tell me, 'You're clean, you're fed, and you've said your prayers. You're good to go.' If they want to laugh, they can do one of two things: Let me know so that I can laugh, too, 'cause I always like a good laugh, or buy me a new suit. Either way is fine by me."

Floyd meant it. He did things his way, and he was always happy. Even more than that, he made other people happy with his consistently positive way of looking at things. He always found the positive in every situation.

"So they laugh at my suits, so what?" he said confidently. "One time I saw some youngsters laughing at my suit when I was at church for a weddin'," he said with his Oklahoma accent shining brightly. "They couldn't have been more than sixteen or seventeen. Just youngin's, that's all. So I put my arms on their shoulders and smiled and told 'em, 'If I would have known it woulda' made ya this happy, I would've worn it yesterday. Glad I could make your day. Enjoy the weddin', y'all.'"

Floyd was glad he could make your day. He believed in three things:

1. Treating others how you want to be treated.
2. Reviewing the positive in every situation, no matter what.
3. Making people laugh when they least expected it with genuine humor and a homegrown Oklahoma way of looking at life.

One time, some months after a member of his church became a widow, Floyd asked her how she was doing. Her name was Hilda, and her husband Harry had passed away after forty-eight years of marriage.

"Ya doin' okay there, Hilda? Anything I can do for ya?" he

asked in his sincere way.

"I'm fine, Floyd. I'm doing fine. Thank you so much for caring."

"Ya know, Hilda, I knew Harry most of m'life. I was at yer weddin' and all, but even I didn't know he was this cheap."

Knowing his child-like sense of humor, she asked him, "What do you mean, Floyd?" Her eyes began to twinkle, and her face had the hint of a smile awaiting his reply.

"Goin' ahead and dyin' and all just so he doesn't have to spend all kinds of money on your fiftieth anniversary. That just takes the cake, Hilda. On a brighter note, that's less socks and underwear ya have to wash."

She burst into laughter and hugged him.

That was his way. He used a genuine sense of humor to touch people's hearts. It was real. It was his "young-at-heart" outlook on life.

After she hugged him, he spent the next twenty minutes or so asking her all sorts of questions about the best memories that she had of Harry, most of which he could guess, but he asked anyway. He listened, and with each answer, he would ask her something else to make her review the positive. He helped her to relive the multitude of blessings and memories that she had shared with Harry through their sixty years of knowing each other and forty-eight years of marriage.

Reviewing the positive was Floyd's key to relationships. One time, one of his friends had a fire that completely destroyed his barn. After the firemen had put the flames out, Floyd stood in front of the ashes and burning embers next to his friend.

Taking his John Deere hat off his head with his right hand, Floyd scratched the top of his head with his left hand, put his hat back on, adjusted it, and said, "Well, at least you don't have to fix the leakin' roof any more. That oughta save ya some time." He actually managed to make his friend chuckle. Floyd was sincere, and he was honest. "There's always something positive in everything," he would say.

Most people underestimated Floyd. They did not give him enough credit for being smart until they got to know him. In 1991, Floyd was still driving his 1974 Ford pickup truck. He would laugh and say, "Didn't want to buy it in '73 'cause I bought my new suits that year." Although he was joking, you knew by his lifestyle that there was a hint of seriousness to his comment.

Floyd was a tomato farmer. He knew just about everything there was to know about tomatoes. He could tell you endless facts and recall crop data from several years earlier. His tomatoes and his church were his life. Most people thought he made his money by selling the tomatoes at stands on street corners. What they did not realize was that he did this for two reasons. First, he wanted to give the high-school children steady work in summer. He could keep them supplied with tomatoes and pay them by the hour. "Keeps 'em off the streets and teaches them the value of a hard-earned dollar," he would say. Second, he donated all of the proceeds from the tomatoes that the high-school workers sold to some type of children's cause, whether it was a kid's cancer fund or some other means to help children.

That is not where Floyd made his money, though. Floyd made his money from vast greenhouses that grew tens of thousands of tomatoes. He was the sole supplier of tomatoes to the grocery stores in his town and to a chain of grocery stores in Oklahoma City. Floyd was an entrepreneur and a very good one. He had personally developed those relationships, secured the business, and nurtured them as clients and as friends the same way that he had nurtured his tomatoes.

"Just don't spray your customers with all kinds of water and chemicals," he would say. "Tomatas kinda like it, but customers get 'bout as sideways as an armadillo in a windstorm on a Texas road. It ain't pretty." Then, he would continue, "Less'n you're a woman. They like all them chemicals and hair things. No pesticides though. Ladies don't like being sprayed with that. Best leave that to the tomatas," he would say with a chuckle.

"Growing relationships is a lot like growing tomatoes," he

often explained as he held up a tomato and examined it. "You have to know what you are doing with both. You wouldn't go back and review what ya did with a batch of tomatoes that didn't grow; you'd go back and review what worked. You would study it. You would get to know how much water you put on 'em, what kinds of bug killer you used, how much sunlight they got, what the temperature was, where you planted 'em, what kinds of fertilizer you used, and the like.

"Growing relationships is a lot like that. It's pretty simple. People don't want to be reminded of the negative things in life. So...don't remind 'em. Always review the positive. Let them know not just that you appreciate them, but what you appreciate about them. And make 'em laugh. Talk about a grasshopper with a wooden leg or a caterpillar on roller skates or something else funny. People like to review the positive, and they like to laugh!"

One time, one of his friends asked him, "What if you can't think of anything funny?"

"Then you're lookin' at life the wrong way, my friend. Life is funny. Can you actually look at a duckbilled platypus and not smile? 'Course ya can't. Just look around you. Funny is when your ma tells you and your brother to use the outhouse before church and you go first and use the toilet paper all up. That's just plain funny." You could always tell by the sincerity of his laughter when he was recalling true memories. "Now that's funny," he said with his shoulders moving up and down as he laughed. "Yep, life's good!"

No one would have guessed that Floyd was such a success without getting to know him. Once you did, you realized that he understood people and relationships. This served him very, very well. Although he drove an old truck, wore overalls, had two outdated suits, and saved money by skipping haircuts, he knew people. He kept his stress low by laughing a lot, and he kept his relationships and subsequent business growing by reviewing the positive.

The key to Floyd's success was in three areas. First, he

understood that he would be happier if he programmed himself to think of the positive and reflect on it, even in negative situations. Second, he was rich with friends because he genuinely cared and always reviewed the positive with them. Third, he was rich with money because he knew the value of it and used it prudently.

As a result of these three things, his business grew. During his life, he was able to loan his church one million dollars in a lump-sum and then forgive the debt. At his death, he left more than three million dollars to charity, none of which was life insurance money; it was all "tomato money." In fact, since he had no wife and no children, he did not even own life insurance.

External Frames of Reference

Floyd never studied the science of neuro-programming in a formal sense. When we had asked him about it, he joked and said, "Must be for city folk." As usual, he was downplaying his excellent ability to grasp concepts and retain information.

So, what is neuro-programming? In short, it is the key to looking for the good and finding it. Quite simply, neuro-programming works by association and repetition. Your mind associates a feeling with a thought. The feeling will be either negative or positive. It is that simple. The more often that you associate "good" with something, the more you program your mind to make that a permanent association.

Floyd understood this over-simplified concept. He wanted people to associate him—his face, and even his name—with feeling good. So, how did he do that? He applied The Rule of 30-45-90 without even knowing that he did. The Rule of 30-45-90 is simple and highly effective. It states:

- If you do something for 30 days, it becomes a habit.
- If you do something for 45 days, it becomes a routine.
- If you do something for 90 days, it becomes a lifestyle.

Clearly Floyd had developed a lifestyle of positive neuro-association through repeated neuro-programming. He consistently taught himself how to look for the good. He did that so often that it became a lifestyle. In other words, he didn't even have to think about it or work hard at it. He just did it. As a result, he always found the good. In turn, he always led others to see the good. Ultimately, everyone began to associate Floyd with finding the good *in* life and feeling good *about* life.

Just as Floyd did, each of us neuro-programs how others feel about us. We program them to associate us with stress, anxiety, and unmet deadlines or with lower stress, peace, and a solid dependency. We program others accidentally or intentionally. By our specific and repetitive interactions, positive or negative, the other individual's subconscious begins to associate us with certain feelings, concepts, or outcomes.

Have you ever had a person not like you from the beginning, and you have no idea why? Accidental and unintentionally negative behavior is the answer. If this behavior is repeated over and over again, you are not building bridges but building walls.

Floyd understood this basic concept and always mentioned the positive. He built many, many bridges with others simply by looking for and finding the good. The Rule of 30-45-90 works because it uses repetition to program our minds. We may think of someone often and thereby have a familiarity with them. However, our actual interactions build upon how they associate us with feeling down and stressed or feeling great and rejuvenated.

As I mentioned, Floyd had one pace—medium. The consistency of his speed complemented the consistent nature of his positive interactions with others. When anyone who knew him at any level—acquaintance or long-time friend—saw Floyd coming, they felt positive and usually smiled before he even greeted them. They had been neuro-programmed to associate him with feeling good.

Once he invited me to ride with him to one of the

supermarket stores in a large chain with which he had exclusive selling rights. As he walked into the store with his cuffed overalls, worn-out striped oxford shirt, handkerchief sticking out of his back pocket, black gardening socks, and John Deere hat, each person that saw him smiled. People's whole face and body posture changed as they greeted him by name.

We made our way back to the manager's office, and Floyd gently tapped on the door. When the manager saw that it was Floyd, he smiled and got up immediately, extending his hand.

"I knew I was coming to see you, so I put on clean socks this morning, can ya tell?" Floyd joked in his lighthearted way. "Woulda changed my underpants, but I did that yesterday," he joked with a smile. "So you'll have to settle for just the socks, Roy."

Roy billowed with laughter almost before Floyd finished speaking. Roy, like so many others, had become so neuro-programmed by Floyd that he just knew Floyd would say something down-to-earth and funny. No doubt when Roy even heard Floyd's name, he would smile or think positive thoughts.

That is the power and impact of positive neuro-programming on our relationships and related outcomes. Floyd understood this at an expert level. Many successful leaders have discovered this ability to connect themselves with positive associations in the minds of others. Let's examine how this is done and why it is so effective.

Twenty years ago, Anthony Robbins stated in his groundbreaking book *Awaken the Giant Within* that individuals by nature either avoid pain or seek pleasure. We are designed to avoid the negative and seek the positive. We are designed to push away, mentally or physically, anything that causes us discomfort, pain, or even inconvenience. We are designed to be attracted to anything that gives us mental or physical comfort, pleasure, or convenience. We often design our interactions, relationships, and environments based on what we are attracted or drawn to. This has very practical applications.

Let's look at another example besides Floyd. All of us have

people in our lives that we don't want to spend much time with. They are like family members that you're as happy to see leave Thanksgiving dinner as you were to see them arrive. This is the type of relationship that I have with Valerie.

I've known Valerie Stevens for years, but I tend to avoid her. Valerie is a downer. No, that's not actually her name, but using her name would not be right, given the references we are going to make.

When I see Valerie, I know the conversation is going to go downhill from wherever it started. Every time I try to bring it back up, she will mention a negative. That is how she chooses to live, so I—and many others who like to look at the positive side of life—choose not to be around her.

Last year I ran into Valerie in the hallway by the office where she works. I was doing consulting work for one of her colleagues. Quite honestly, I felt like the Pink Panther or Austin Powers as I peeked around the corner to see if she was there. I don't enjoy talking with her and will do whatever I can to avoid her. Every attempt that I have made to give her a positive attitude has been met with the resistance of a jackrabbit being boarded at a dog kennel during feeding time. It just never has gone well.

This particular day, I was checking to make sure she was nowhere to be seen because I had to visit the office across from hers. I felt the coast was clear as I made my way past her office. I did so quickly and quietly so as not to bring attention to myself. With her office on my right and the office I needed to visit on my left, I watched over my right shoulder as I turned to quickly enter the office of my client. As fate would have it, I was greeted by the words, "I was just thinking about you."

It was Valerie.

I had run right into her, literally. This is no small deal when you consider that I am 5'8" and about 160 pounds and she is 5'8" and about 260 pounds. I bounced off her like a rubber ball off a brick wall. She giggled with delight at finding someone with whom to share the dismal emotional weather forecast of her life. She would express this while reviewing in great detail the carnal wreckage that past events had dealt to her.

"Hi, Valerie," I said with a smile. Never, I mean, never do I ask her, "How is it going?" That would be like asking Abraham Lincoln's widow, "Besides that, Mrs. Lincoln, how did you like the play?" No good answer was going to result, no matter how the question was asked.

"Hi, Chris, so what's new?" she asked ritualistically as if it was polite. In reality, it only set the stage for her to share her downcast stories. No matter how optimistic or positive my answer, I knew she was saying to herself, *Okay, set…spike…score…game point…victory*! as if she were playing emotional volleyball and would do anything possible to end on a negative note.

"Life is good!" I said. "Lot's of good things happening."

"I wish you could tell my husband that…" she said with a pregnant pause that invited me to ask "why?"

No way. I was not going to do it. I have removed that fishhook before, and I was not taking the bait this time.

"I'm sure he will find the positive," I confidently assured her.

"Ha!" she replied in total disagreement. "He still doesn't have his new contract for work since his company was bought out, and the stress is really starting to get to him. He's yelling at the kids. My daughter is a wreck. Oh, by the way, did I tell you that she is pregnant?"

"Congratulations!" I responded.

"Chris," she replied with the authority of a teacher explaining that two plus two does not equal five. "You do know that she is a junior in high school, don't you?"

"A grandma?" I retorted with excitement, putting up a "Road Closed for Repair" sign in the conversation and redirecting the traffic of our discourse down "Pleasant Valley Road."

"I know. It reminds me that I am getting older… as if my body giving out did not do that already."

"You are only as old as you feel," I said confidently.

"In that case, I am close to being six feet under."

The conversation went for what seemed like five minutes going on two hours. Then, she did the unthinkable: She placed her left leg on the corner of the table in the hallway and eased down to sit on it. This meant she was going to stay a while. In the words of Barney Fife, I decided to "nip it in the bud…just nip it in the bud." I told her that I really needed to go because I had a meeting across the hall.

"Stop by on your way out," she said. "We can finish our conversation. I have a lot more to share."

Oh, I'm sure you do, I thought to myself. *Everyone else's emotional landfill has been used, and you need new dumping grounds.*

"I really have to run afterwards," I explained. "I have a tight day!"

"Me, too," she confirmed. "In fact, I don't know how I'm going to get everything done. But that's nothing new. I'm just supposed to smile and buckle down."

Smile? I thought. *Smile?* As we ended this conversation, I turned and entered my client's office.

"Sorry I am a few minutes late," I apologized. "I ran into Valerie."

The responses ranged from, "Oh no!" to "I'm sorry!" to "Yes, we figured you did. She just left here…and you're still smiling?"

I thought how sad it was. None of these people were being mean. None of them meant any ill will toward her. Just the opposite was true. They wanted her to be happy and had made every conceivable attempt, even inconveniencing themselves, to brighten her spirits.

All their attempts had failed. Valerie had decided, at some point in her life, to have a pessimistic outlook. She chose to subject others to it involuntarily, like giving someone a building site downwind from a manure pile. It wasn't a pleasant experience, no matter how you constructed it.

You may be thinking that perhaps she is clinically depressed or has some other condition. This could be true, but I finally said to her, "Valerie. You always seem down, and I want to help you. Before you explain why your current challenges have you down, I would like to make you an offer. Let me help you by redirecting your focus. I do this all the time in private consultations for individuals who want to redirect, and it works wonderfully. If I cannot help you, I guarantee you that we can find someone who can."

Her response said it all. "I doubt it," she said with a sincere but immovable tone. "I just have to work through it myself, I guess."

"Well, Valerie. The offer still stands."

"Thanks, Chris."

"However, Valerie, if you do not take me up on my offer, I am not interested in hearing about things that I cannot fix. Again, I will help you through or lead you to someone who can, but I really do not want to be helpless in the face of your challenges. It is not a fun place to be, Valerie. Just let me know if I can help."

She agreed even though I knew that she would not take me up on it. At the very least, I had sold my downwind parcel of land and moved to more pleasant pastures of human interaction. She remains very nice to me to this day whenever I see her. However, she no longer engages in long conversations. Others, however, are still dealing with what many have termed "Valerie Syndrome." That is their way of stating that she will not change and that even the mention of her name brings them down.

Accentuate the Positive

Clearly Floyd and Valerie are opposites in their internal perspectives and the resulting human interactions. Floyd was well liked and the mention of his name still brings smiles to our faces as we write this book. Valerie is hard to like because you cannot see past her never-ending troubles, and the mention of her name brings a negative association. Both individuals have consistently and effectively neuro-programmed those around them. Each person has successfully neuro-associated themselves in others' minds with either pain or pleasure.

Is it that simple? You bet.

The mind works much like a computer. In fact, the circuitry of computers is said to have been developed based on our knowledge of how the human brain works. The more we learn about our brain, the better we are able to build more efficient and effective computers. In much the same way, when we learn how the human brain works and how it stores information, we can create more effective and productive relationships.

We have to start with the outcomes we want to achieve. That ties directly to how we want to be viewed by others and the associations we want to create in their minds. This takes conscious effort. If we build a positive mindset, we will not have to work so arduously on creating positive interactions. They will come as second nature. But we have to start by developing that positive mental outlook and internal frame of reference. Remember, it's not what you see, but how you choose to see it that counts. In closing, I invite you to:

- Look for the good in yourself.
- Look for the good in others.
- Look for the good in your situation.
- Look for the good in life.

Life truly is good, if we choose to look for the good!

CHAPTER 7

GENTLEMEN, START YOUR SCOOTERS

LEARN TO LIGHTEN UP AND STAY IN MOTION

There is a reason why people who laugh are healthier than those who don't. Laughing is good for you physically. It changes your mental state. It changes the way that you interact with others. Most of all, it keeps things in perspective.

This allows us to find the good even when situations are challenging. If we consistently learn to laugh at life during everyday occurrences, we can learn how to handle difficult times with greater success. Let me share an example of how an ordinary experience can change your mood when you look at it with a fun perspective. This event happened while we were still living in Wisconsin prior to moving to Tennessee.

In addition to owning two cars, we have a Honda Metropolitan motor scooter. It is small and fun and goes about 35 miles per hour at maximum speed. It is easy to handle and can fit just about anywhere. With Wisconsin winter soon approaching, I was enjoying the last few days of autumn riding. This particular day, I was riding to and from the health club a few miles from our house.

While riding home, I focused on enjoying my day and having fun. As I approached a stoplight not far from my destination, I noticed two motorcycles waiting side-by-side at the light. They were both "super bikes," those shiny, sleek motorcycles that can go more than 140 miles an hour while the riders lean forward like racers.

The bike on the left was flashy red. It had a silver lightning bolt running down the side and two large tailpipes on either side of the small racing seat. The driver was wearing a black-and-red leather racing jacket, black leather gloves, and a red helmet. His helmet had a black face shield and a silver lighting bolt on either side. He was revving the engine, and the heat coming from the tailpipes made optical waves in the air.

The bike on the right was all black and tough. The word "Ninja" was painted on the gas tank. The rider was dressed all in black. He wore a black leather racing jacket that said "Ninja" on the back. He had on black pants, black racing boots, black gloves, and a black shiny helmet with a darkened face shield. The side of the helmet just said "Ninja." He too had heat waves coming from the hot exhaust pipes being driven by the bike's racing engine.

This should be good for a laugh, I thought to myself. I saw just enough space to pull up between them. As I approached them, my scooter made a sound very much like the train that went to the Land of Make-Believe on the *Mister Rogers' Neighborhood* TV show.

I eased slowly up to them with my feet walking my scooter forward—left, right, left, right, left, right. My shiny, white Nikes pounded the pavement with an ominous thud as I slowed the scooter to the line. I approached them like a bad outlaw biker challenging the pack. My scooter is white and power blue, and roughly one-fourth the size of their motorcycles. (Hey, I got a good deal on it, and my kids liked the color.)

Anyway, as my white Nikes walked the scooter forward, I made my presence known. In my mind, I heard my Nikes hit the concrete with the toughness and intimidation of an inmate's shoes on a second-story, grated-metal prison floor. To quote an old George Thorogood song, I felt "bad to the bone."

Left. Right. Left. Right. Left. Right.

Pound. Pound. Pound. Pound. Pound. Pound.

I couldn't prove it, but I think the earth was shaking. Maybe it was me, because the scooter is a one-person, 50cc moped-like vehicle.

As I approached them, I got my game on. I could feel the wind whipping against my chest, but I was tough as nails. I could take anything. Sure, the temperature had dropped to a chilly sixty-five degrees with the wind bringing just a hint of autumn scent from the northwest. But with my Ralph Lauren tan-and-beige argyle golf shirt, I owned the road. I defined toughness.

As I coasted to an intimidating stop, I stood up slowly with a short, yet commanding presence. With total confidence, I fixed the scooter wedgie that I had experienced for the past four miles. As I sat down, I felt like I owned the road. I felt the shocks on the front of the scooter groan as I lowered my massive five-foot-eight, one-hundred-fifty-pound frame to the seat. I slowly adjusted the strap on my Trek bicycle helmet. It was black—tough guy black—with the intimidating word "Trek" on the side.

Slowly, I squeezed the left brake. I had the iron grip of a member of Heck's Angels. Bear with me. I can't very well say Hell's Angels on a powder-blue scooter, can I?

I revved the engine to make my presence known. Even though my scooter gets 100 mpg, I could hear the gas money getting sucked recklessly through the engine and being blown out the scooter's tiny tailpipe. I was going to command their attention. They would be shaking in their biker boots.

Nothing.

Their racing engines were the only sound around. They ruled the intersection. Out of the corner of my eye, I could see that the guy on my right had a tattoo of a knife on his wrist between where his glove stopped and his jacket started.

You wanna play, mister tough guy? I thought to myself.

I slowly reached back and adjusted my briefcase under the blue bungee cords. The mild acceleration of the scooter could make my Day-Timer wrinkle inside the briefcase. I may be tough and reckless, but I am sensible.

I've got game, buddy. Bring it on, I thought to myself as I turned back to face forward now that my briefcase was firmly fastened.

This time I locked the front brake and really revved that little bugger to the max. My left mirror was shaking like a nervous autumn leaf or like Barney Fife when he thinks there's trouble. Upon hearing the revving sound come from my scooter, the guy on my left looked around to see if it was a mosquito or a bee.

As I went to release the brake, I accidentally bumped the horn. It sounded just like the Road Runner from *The Bugs Bunny/Road Runner Hour*. However, it made me feel fast and invincible.

At this, the driver on the left looked over and saw me.

I smiled.

He laughed, appreciating the intended humor I was trying to convey.

I revved.

He revved.

I revved louder.

He revved louder.

I was maxed out on revving. I started to hear the voice of Scottie from the original *Star Trek* saying (insert Scottish accent), "Aye, Captain! It is just no use! She can't take any more! She's given all she's got, man! Have mercy." My engine was making the sputtering sound that a Toro lawnmower makes just before it runs out of gas.

I nodded.

I looked to the right. His friend on my right was laughing, too.

I looked at the light. It had not yet changed.

I released the brake enough to edge forward like I meant business. To show my reckless intent, I reaching down and opened one more button on my argyle golf shirt.

I definitely meant business.

The wind had accelerated to a gusty twelve miles per hour, but I was tough. The light changed, and the motorcycles increased the temperature around my scooter by twenty degrees with the rocket-like thrust through their exhaust pipes. I saw taillights and heard them leave with the velocity of F-16 fighter jets.

I'll be waiting, boys. Oh, I'll be waiting... I said to myself as my scooter started across the intersection at full acceleration. It sounded like the engine of a remote-control model airplane. Once again, I had the road to myself.

This story illustrates a point. I love to laugh. I am a firm believer that it makes us happier and healthier and brings greater quality to our lives. More people should take a comedic look at life at least once a day. My suggestion is: Take time to daydream—and make the daydream fun. Make up the interaction as I did, and make yourself laugh. If you do, you will train yourself to think that way.

But as I laughed at the fun that those guys and I had, I rode and continued to think about drive and motion. I began to think not just about the humor of their speed vs. mine, but about movement in general. They were like the rabbit in "The Tortoise and the Hare," and I was like the tortoise.

Water over the Dam and Progressive Motion

As I continued to ride home, I paused to observe the Milwaukee River flowing over a dam in the town where we lived. I noticed the clarity of the water. While we lived in this town, I'd seen times when the river moved slowly and times after rain when the river moved swiftly toward, and then over, the dam. I started to wonder why the water was so pure and clear, why it looked so beautiful as it splashed over the dam and foamed at the bottom. The answer was because of the movement of the water.

We lived in an area that is beautiful with upscale homes and developments but also close to nature preserves with trails and ponds on the edge of Lake Michigan. As I looked at the water, I thought of another body of water that I had seen not much earlier. During summer, my family and I were hiking in the forest preserve. My children are small enough that we enjoy trying to spot the green frogs on top of the leaves and moss in the pond. As we searched for frogs, I noticed the thick moss and bright green color of the water. It was stagnant because it had not moved all summer.

As I rode home, I thought about the contrast between that stagnant, mossy pond water and the clear, pure water going over the dam. Each was beautiful in its own way as part of nature, but as I thought about the ideas that we were trying to express related to personal excellence, I kept coming back to the dam. People want to be around clear water. Stagnant water is great if you are a frog trying to blend in, but not if you are a person.

The clear water seemed to never stop, as if there was an endless supply and the river would constantly be cleansed while providing beauty and power. Movement and progress were the keys to the clarity of the water.

In much the same way, I started to think about movement and progress in our lives. I thought of how, when we cease to move forward, we become stagnant. And how, when we cease to make improvement or even strive to higher levels of excellence, we end up being like that pond water. We end up not going much of anywhere and not doing much of anything.

In contrast, I thought of how as we continue to drive and engage our life, we continue to purify our intentions. Much like how that water was purified, as we continue to move forward and produce actions and movement, we stay fresh. This actually makes others take notice. Our movement engages them. And that movement doesn't always have to be physical. It can be intellectual or emotional. Even then, it doesn't have to be monumental or significant. My interaction with the bikers at the stoplight wasn't monumental or significant, but it engaged us for a brief moment with enough laughter to make our day.

I serve as a coach in a variety of areas, in addition to coaching our kids' sports teams. I serve as a life coach for individuals seeking clarity and focus. I serve as a business coach for those who want to draw on the ideas of other individuals, and I serve as a strategic planning coach for individuals who want to take their company or group to the next level. I also serve as an executive coach for individuals who head companies or organizations and need a confidential, non-political, non-biased ear to give feedback.

Recently, one of my clients asked me the same question that he asks in nearly every coaching session. To start the session, he called me. Almost immediately after I answered the phone and we exchanged greetings, Tim posed the recurring question.

"Chris, before we get into what I'd like to talk about today, I have an important question for you. I want you to give me the straightforward answer, regardless of what it is."

"Tim," I said, "I always give you the straightforward answer, and I always listen with an ear for your agenda. That's what being a coach is all about."

"I know," he said, "but I'm really nervous about the answer to this question, and I don't want you to say something just to make me feel good."

"You have my word," I said, fully knowing what question was coming next. I knew he was going to ask me about the amount of progress he felt he was making in comparison to other individuals I have coached and continue to coach. I paused, waited, and could almost mouth the words with him.

"Chris, in your professional experience as a seasoned, veteran executive coach, am I making the same kind of progress as other individuals? Or am I falling behind?"

My answer was what I tell him each time he asks. I said, "Tim, please do not compare yourself to other people. There is no 'ahead of other people' or 'behind other people.' When I became an executive coach, one of the first things I learned was to take everyone at the stage where they are. That advice would serve you well. You are where you should be, and, yes, you are making tremendous progress. The important thing is that you continue to create a motion in your life—a motion of progress."

I could hear the sigh of relief at the other end of the phone, which usually is followed by the need for reaffirmation.

"Are you sure? Coming from you that means a lot."

"I am sure," I said, and with that, we continued our conversation.

I raise this point for a good reason. The fact that Tim wanted to ensure that he was making progress told me a great deal about his intentions. His drive meant he wanted to arrive at a place that was better than before. His drive meant that he was seeking to arrive somewhere different, and he wanted to make sure he was on track.

Wanting to compare himself to others was unnecessary, but natural, because he had no other benchmark and he was using me as a sounding board. Once I redirected him, he was once again operating at the speed he needed to be. Whatever progress he was making was the right progress for him.

As we examine the concept of progressive motion in our lives, I would encourage you to take the same view that I encouraged him to take:

- Do not compare yourself to others in terms of what you have or have not accomplished in life.
- Do not compare yourself and where you want to go, to where you are now. Instead, look at what you have accomplished and where you have come from.
- Do not even compare yourself to what you could have done or should have done. Compare yourself only to the progress you have made and where you want to go.

Think of this book as a coaching manual. While I was completing my doctoral studies in psychotherapy and human interaction, I learned a big difference between psychotherapy and coaching. Therapy looks backward to determine what could have been done differently so that those mistakes can be avoided going forward. Coaching looks back to celebrate the positives that have occurred and see how they can be repeated or replicated going forward. I encourage you to take the coaching approach and look forward.

As we look at the concept of drive, we have to ask ourselves, what are we driving to? What are we moving toward? This is a way of casting our vision and establishing who and what will be in our future. As we do this and make progress toward including the people and things in our future that will bring our vision into reality, we need to ask what we are moving toward within that vision. In other words, how are we positioning ourselves with others for increased progress and success as we make our vision a reality? I suggest to you that we are moving toward service and success.

This book is called *It's Not Rocket Surgery* because we are not trying to reinvent the wheel. We are simply taking concepts, ideas, and techniques that have worked well for thousands of people and putting them together in one concise, easy-to-read manual.

Many of the concepts are ones you have heard before but may need to revisit. We have all heard advice from people. Much of it is bad, but some of it is good. We are here to filter out the noise and tell you what really works. We have done the hard part, conducting the research and developing the strategies that work. All you have to do is apply these concepts to your life.

Service in Motion on the Road to Success

As I mentioned, as we position ourselves to make our vision a reality, we are moving toward service. This concept can be expressed in many ways, some of which seem clichéd but ring true. One of those is: We give to live. Or: We achieve the greatest success by serving. Many personal excellence trainers say: The extent to which we provide needed or wanted service to other individuals determines the extent to which we will experience our own success.

If we examine any industry, we can see that this is true. In our industry, for example, our business only grows as we serve more people through coaching, training, and consulting. Before we talk about service leading to success, though, let's understand what we mean by those two terms.

Service can be defined as "helpful activities" or "assistance to those who need it." Helpful activity means supplying a thought, action, or thing someone needs or wants to achieve his or her goal, or make progress toward it. In many industries, two businesses will work together so they can both get ahead. The idea of "I rub your back, and you rub mine," is a good starting point. That is motion toward cooperation.

When we reach out in service, to give and not get back, though, the results are amazing and we get back more than we thought. For example, our homes look much more comfortable and spacious after a trip to a third-world country, and food tastes much better after we volunteer to feed the homeless. You don't have to look far or even go outside your comfort zone to find a way to be of service. You can put service into motion wherever you are.

That leads to the next word: success. Success can be defined as "favorable results from efforts" or "the attainment of goals." We often think of success as simply including incredible wealth, record-breaking athletic activity, high position with a great title, or creation of an invention that changes the world. I don't deny that any of these represents success, but I think they provide a very narrow definition of it.

We have studied super-success in the United States and throughout the world. Based on that research, we believe—and our experience has shown—that success can be best described as *progress towards a worthwhile goal.* Progress, by its very nature, includes motion. In the personal excellence seminars that we conduct, we often tell participants, "As we talk about success and the super-successes of our culture, I would like you to tell me who two people are. Fair enough?

"Fair enough," they respond.

"Who is Bill Gates?" I ask.

They usually answer with one word: "Microsoft!" Followed by a second word: "Rich!"

I ask, "Is he wealthy, yes or no?"

"Yes!" they say, usually grinning or giggling at the amount of money he has.

"Is he successful, yes or no?" I ask. "Yes!" they all say loudly in unison.

As I pace the stage, I look at the crowd and ask, "Who was Mother Teresa?" The responses usually are: "Saint!" and "Missionary!"

"Was she wealthy or poor?" I ask. "Very poor!" they say in unison.

"Was she successful, yes or no?" I say. And a resounding, "Yes!" comes back in a unified voice almost louder than for Bill Gates.

Then I make the point that success may or may not involve large sums of money, power, or position. Success is progress towards a worthwhile goal. If an individual's goal is to lose fifteen pounds in a month, and they lose only eight ounces a day, they are successful, right?

If we look at success as "progress towards a worthwhile goal," and service as "helpful activity," we can see the connection. When we engage our drive and create motion in our lives, the amount of success we experience will result from the amount of service we give. Saying it another way: The amount of progress we make toward a worthwhile goal will relate to how much help we have been giving.

When we look at engaging our drive, we can start from either service or success, depending on our outlook and our purpose. If our purpose is material reward—to get as much as we can of status, popularity, money, or position, we are going to give service in exchange for a promotion, being paid, or status. That means we need to continually seek ways to put our product, service, or name in front of others to meet their purposes.

Likewise, if our purpose is to give as much back as we can to the world, we are going to go the extra mile and put our product, service, or name toward helping as many people as possible and not necessarily ourselves. We want to move further along, to get more, do more, or be more. In doing so, we may gain one or more of the following: strong reputation, status or promotion, or financial rewards.

People who act out of service, not simply for reward, are generally viewed as more open, friendly, and honest. This, in turn, creates relationships and opportunities for them to continually experience increasing levels of progress. The purpose in your life will bring you the energy to keep going toward your goal. Others will notice the self-esteem you gain by completing the small steps along the way and be inspired by you. Your self-confidence will increase with the more energy that you set in motion, the more service that you give, and the more responses that you get from others. This is a cycle that will feed on itself.

As you engage your drive, don't misunderstand the concept of service. Service does not have to mean giving endlessly until we are exhausted in hope that we made a difference in the world or the lives of others. As we have spoken to physicians, nurses, and other health-care providers across the country, we have seen "service to exhaustion," particularly in the medical profession. We have also seen this in the teaching profession.

These professionals believe so deeply in what they provide and the difference they can make that they sometimes give until they're exhausted. While this is admirable, it can be more of an energy drain than an energy producer. We share with these professionals that taking downtime and being rested will help them to provide greater service.

At the same time, service does not mean that we have to give our talents and abilities away for free or next to nothing. We have seen many people in social service organizations who believe in helping others at their own expense. This can be a dangerous trap, with family members paying the price. Service also does not stand in the way of being profitable. In some situations, just the opposite may be true. Self-development companies and professionals, for example, are quite profitable. Many of them gauge the amount of service that they have provided by the amount of revenue that they generate. In fact, some of them look at the revenue as receipts for service provided. They are most often in business to serve, but their service produces returns for them.

Being of service to others is good for us and keeps us in motion. Having fun and laughing at life while we are being of service is equally important. You can gauge your attitude on life and your progress (or motion) in life by asking yourself the following questions:

Attitude Questions

- Have I taken the time to laugh today?
- What have I looked for and found that is good in my life today?
- Have I focused on something that makes me smile?
- What good can I expect in my life and look forward to tomorrow or the next day?
- What can I do today to help make that good event take place?

Motion Questions

- Have I improved myself in some way today?
- Have I improved my outlook in some way today?
- What have I learned today that is new?
- What can I do today to improve my life tomorrow?
- Have I put positive and valuable information in my mind today?

Each of us will laugh more on some days than on others. Each of us will be in motion or make more progress on some days than on others. The point is to make these things happen regularly—and more often. If we focus on finding things in life to laugh about or smile at, we will find them. They are all around us. The more we look for them, the easier they are to see. In my example, I could have ridden my scooter home with no interaction with the two gentlemen on the motorcycles, but where is the fun in that? I gave them a good laugh, and I had a good laugh.

Clear Out the Clutter in Your Mental Hard Drive

As simple as it sounds, laughing gives us perspective. It keeps us balanced. It helps us to keep our eye on the bigger picture. After all, by letting things bother us, we give them more weight than they should have and spend more time thinking about them. When we choose instead to look at things that are good, right, positive, and downright funny, we keep our focus more positive. And the more often we focus on the positive, the easier it becomes to do so. While we may have to think about it at first, over time it becomes a natural thought process.

Why is this important? That is a great question! It is important because when we replace our focus on negative experiences and outcomes with a focus on things that are positive, and at times even funny, we free up space on our hard drive, so to speak. A computer's hard drive has only so much space available at any time. If you have clutter on your hard drive, you'll run out of space eventually for what you want or need to store there. So, what do you do? You erase the clutter and fill that storage area with the positive things that you need. In doing so, you often find that you have more space than you thought and can access important things easier.

Our mind works very much the same way. When you eliminate concerns that you don't need to be concerned about, or worries that you don't need to worry about, you free up space in your mind. You can use this freed space to look at the good in life. You can find the good and funny things around you easier. You may not have seen them before because you had too much clutter—negative thoughts or worry that took your attention. The more often you remove the clutter, the more natural it becomes to see the good in life. It becomes part of who you are.

As you begin to switch your focus and lighten up, you set yourself in motion. The motion is called progress. And as you begin to look for the good things in life, you'll also look for ways to expand your thinking and shape your attitude. For example, I haven't watched local news on television in more than twenty years. I am not uninformed or keeping myself in the dark. I simply choose not to surround myself with the negativity that they report on. I can just as easily pick up a newspaper and read it.

What's the difference? I can't dictate what anchors and reporters will say on the news. I know most of it will be negative. Quite frankly, I don't need to surround myself with that, especially if it doesn't involve me or involves others that I cannot help. Instead, I can glance at a newspaper and determine quickly whether an article is positive or negative. If it is negative, I can determine if it affects me or if I can do something about it. If so, I read the article. If not, I skip over it.

This keeps me in motion. Think about it. Instead of watching thirty minutes or an hour of mostly negative news, I get all the positive news I want in just a few moments. I have taken clutter out of my day and can focus on reading or listening to something that will help my progress.

You can do the same! In fact, by reading this book, you are doing that right now. Congratulations. You could be watching the news or something else negative. Keep doing these types of activities to expand your mind, and use your mental storage space, if you will, for good and positive things. The sooner you start to lighten up, the sooner you will set yourself in positive motion and the more progress you will make.

Just remember, as you continue on your journey to personal excellence: Look both ways before you cross the street of life because those powder-blue scooters are fast!

CHAPTER 8

POODLES, OVERALLS, AND SAMMY HAGAR

IN COMMUNICATION WITH OTHERS, TIMING IS EVERYTHING

As Julie and I undertook our quest to understand personal excellence and high-performance leadership, we studied many different people. You can learn much by doing this, but you often learn the most by examining your own personal excellence and high-performance leadership.

Please remember that we are also on this personal journey. Each day we work to remember our own journey. There is nothing like owning your own business to keep you focused on staying in motion and being of service. In doing so, you can compare what you should have done or said to what others have done or said more effectively in a similar situation. A couple of examples come to mind, such as that of Amy, our neighbor in Fort Wayne, Indiana.

When Julie and I were in the second year of our marriage and I was in my fourth year of graduate school, we moved into an apartment complex not far from the school. In fact, many of the married graduate students lived there.

I guess you would actually call this a townhouse complex, rather than an apartment complex. Each building had ten or twelve different units set next to each other. Each unit shared walls to the sides with the next, and each had outside entrances to the front and back and a fenced-in backyard with a gate. They were cozy, compact, inexpensive, and just the ticket for a couple finishing school.

They also were a government cooperative, so not everyone

who lived there was a student. Some tenants were single people or families who, for whatever reason, did not make a tremendous amount of money. That was fine with us. We get along with everyone and would be moving in a year when I graduated. Still, we wanted to make friends, even if only for a year.

When we arrived, I decided to meet our neighbors and start off on the right foot. Whenever I saw any of them outside, I would walk over, offer a friendly handshake, and introduce myself. During the first couple of days, Julie and I managed to introduce ourselves to almost everyone. We have always liked to take a lot of walks, so this made it easier.

We had met our neighbor to the north who was getting engaged soon and welcomed us to the neighborhood. However, we still had not met our neighbor to the south. At first we thought she was out of town because all of her window shades were drawn and there were no signs of life. Then, we noticed that her car was there at certain times but not at others. Therefore, she had to be home.

"Perhaps she's shy," I said to Julie.

"Perhaps she wants to be left alone," she suggested.

"Left alone is one thing," I admitted, "but living in a cave is sort of strange."

"It's different from you, but that doesn't make it strange," she responded.

"You've got me there. It's different, but I think I'll go and introduce myself," I said happily.

"Why don't you wait until she is outside?" Julie suggested.

"No way; where's the fun in that?" I asked sarcastically.

"Fun is only fun if both people are having fun," she said. This phrase is so true. She has taught it to our children very well. I would like to teach it to many of the drivers I have encountered in Chicago, but that's another story.

"Why do you think I should wait?"

"Because," she contributed, "if someone keeps their shades down all the time and you never see them, they might be kind of private."

"Never see them?" I asked. "It's only been two days."

"That makes my point even more. Give it time."

Keep in mind that we had just finished our first year of marriage. I was young and dumb. Now, twenty years into our relationship, I have a different understanding. I now know that if I ignore Julie's advice when it isn't a matter of life or death and doesn't involve safety issues, it will come back to bite me in the britches like a Texas termite.

"I'm going to go over there and introduce myself," I said with great determination. "After all, it's just me. What's not to like about me?"

Julie just stood at the kitchen counter and continued to cut the potatoes we were cooking for dinner.

"Okay," she skeptically replied with her voice rising at the end. I have since come to know that tone of voice as, "When you get bitten in the britches like a Texas termite, I promise not to say 'I told you so.' "

I left to go next door with all the confidence of a motivational speaker. "Next door" was only the thickness of a wall from our front door.

I knocked on the door.

Nothing.

I waited.

Nothing.

I knocked again.

All of the townhouses had the same standard equipment, a lock on the doorknob and a deadbolt, so I found it odd when I heard a deadbolt unlock—and then another. Then I heard a third. Then the doorknob opened. The door was still chained, so it only opened about four inches.

There she stood. I am not sure which Dean Koontz novel she is in, but she is in there. I think the book is titled, "Quirky."

She said nothing.

I said, "Hi."

She said nothing.

Awkward silence.

I said, "Hi."

She said nothing.

More awkward silence.

"Hi!" I said smiling. "I'm your new neighbor, Chris Irelan. My wife Julie and I just moved in." I didn't dare put out my hand for fear of having it lobbed off by a fast-shutting door. So instead, I just stood and waved. Thinking back, I looked like a kindergartner or Gomer Pyle. I felt like reciting a Gomer Pyle line and saying something like, "Cousin Goober says, 'Hay!' "

The door shut.

More drawn-out, awkward silence.

Then I heard the chain rattle. The door opened about a foot. There stood what had to be Captain Kangaroo's sister. I kid you not. She had the same hair—straight down, bowl cut, and she wore the sides like female sideburns. She had on bib overalls and was shaped like Mr. Potato Head. I don't say this with malice or ill intent. I am no one to judge anyone, trust me. However you need to get the same visuals as I did to get the humor and understand the main points of what I have to share.

"Hi," she said in the same monotone voice that Tyne Daly's character, Mary Beth Lacey, used in the television show *Cagney & Lacey* when she wanted to show a complete absence of emotion or approval.

I repeated myself. "Hi, I'm Chris Irelan, and I just..."

"I heard you the first time," she interrupted in the same monotone.

More awkward silence.

Okeedookee then, I thought to myself.

More awkward silence.

Under her overalls, she wore a short-sleeved shirt that looked exactly like the one worn by the cartoon character Charlie Brown. It had the same horizontal lines. She had on pink socks and sneakers like those my future daughter would wear…when she was three. Each panel of the sneaker was a different color.

"Name's Amy."

She said it with the same lack of emotion. She sounded as if she were answering a police interrogation. I felt like responding in the same tone, *Okay, Miss Happy Feet. How long have you lived here, and what's your deal?* Instead, I cleared my throat and said, "Hi, Amy!"

I noticed, quite by accident, that she had no pictures on her walls and boxes in her apartment like she had just moved in.

"Have you lived here long?" I asked, trying to break the silence.

"Nine years."

"Oh, well, I just wanted to introduce myself to you. Listen, we're easygoing people and aren't really wild or anything," I said, making the same type of expressions and body contortions as Steve Martin in his "Wild and Crazy Guy" routine. That's just who I am. I am animated.

Amy wasn't amused. Anyone watching would have thought the two of us looked really funny, me bopping around imitating "wild and crazy," while she stood there like a statue of Kathy Bates from Stephen King's movie *Misery*. Her body was motionless, and her eyes just followed me.

No expression. Her arms hung straight down at her sides.

My goofy laughter started to slow down. It halted to a clearing of the throat. "Hey, listen, I just wanted to make sure that my stereo didn't bother you or anything, because..."

"Stereo?" she interrupted with the physical force of a Texas wind shear. I had a vision of myself flying backwards horizontally as if I were holding onto a flagpole or tree to keep from flying away. She had spoken voluntarily. I felt like responding like Gene Wilder's character in *Young Frankenstein*: "*She lives! She's alive, I tell you! ALIVE*!" (Insert mad scientist laughter for effect.)

"What stereo?" she asked.

"The one I have in the apartment," I said, pointing reluctantly over my shoulder. I had the feeling that I had just opened a can of worms—and they were attack worms. "Yeah, I (pause), uh, I (clearing throat), uh, just wanted to make sure it doesn't bother you.

"Let's find out."

I could hear that old-time Western whistle (whooheehooo) that indicates there's going to be a standoff.

"Excuse me?" I said, hoping I had heard wrong.

"Go put it on," she said, "and I will listen from my apartment."

I was a clean-cut graduate student finishing a master's degree and headed for doctoral studies. I am about as straight-laced as they come, yet I am sure I heard her say, *Go put it on, rocker boy*! But only the words, "Go put it on," managed to escape past her gritted teeth.

"Okay, I'll be right back," I said. Meanwhile, I was saying to myself, *What have I done? What have I done? What have I done? What have I done*? I went back and told Julie what I was doing.

Her response was, "What have you done?"

I booted up our 250-watt Kenwood receiver that fed power through a "monster cable" into Cerwin Vega D-9s that could rip the shingles off a second-story roof. We had purchased the system a year earlier, and the regular speaker cables weren't enough for Chris Irelan, oh no.

I looked through our CDs. Let's see, Def Leppard, U2, Van Halen, Roxette, Sammy Hagar. Ah, ha! Just the ticket, Ludwig von Beethoven: *Missa Solemnis.* (Insert radio announcer voice: "He shoots! He scores!") I put it in and placed the volume on 2.5 out of 20. Ahhh, yesss. I walked out the front door with the confidence of a teenager who had just passed a driving test. I was going places. I had dug a hole by going over there, but I had leapt out with the power of an Olympic athlete by finding *Missa Solemnis.*

I walked next door. Her door was open. She was actually inside with her ear pressed to the wall. *You've got to be kidding*, I thought to myself.

"Nope, too loud. It simply won't do."

The hole had become a grave with a one-year lease. "That's too loud?" I asked in shock and disbelief.

"If I can hear it, it's too loud."

"But the walls are thin and our apartments are connected."

"If I can hear it, it's too loud."

"It's not on all the time."

"If I can hear it, it's too loud."

Awkward silence.

"I'll tell you what, Amy...can I call you Amy?" I asked in my best salesman voice, looking for the natural affirmative.

"It's a free world," she said with the softness of a drill sergeant.

"Amy, I'll work on it," I said in a compromising tone.

"If I can hear it, it's too loud."

"Okay then. Well, listen, it's been great meeting you, and I look forward to seeing you around," I said with the same feeling as saying it to a sheriff's deputy who had just handed me a ticket for reckless driving because I was doing twenty-seven miles an hour in a twenty-five-mile-an-hour zone.

Julie was kind enough to take the encounter with laughter and said, "Well, look, it's only a year, not even that. I am sure we can work something out." She hadn't met Captain Kangaroo's psycho sister. I prayed for the best.

A few weeks later, two of our good friends, Darryl and Kristen, were over to watch a movie after the four of us had gone out to dinner. In the car, I had been telling him about our neighbor. Darryl's response was a loving, "Better you than me, bro. Better you than me." Kristen and Julie thought it was funny and quirky at the same time.

"What's up with the boxes?" I asked rhetorically. "Nine years and still boxes; that's just odd."

"Different, not odd," Julie offered.

"No, that's just strange," said Darryl, laughing.

Back at our apartment, we got settled in and ready to watch

the movie. We were watching the first *Batman* with Michael Keaton and Kim Basinger. It was fun, entertaining, and fast moving. We were keeping it down so Amy wouldn't get upset.

At one point, however, we simply couldn't hear it. Meaning well, Darryl got up to turn it up a bit. He did not realize that it was a 250-watt Kenwood receiver with monster cables running into Cerwin Vega D-9s. As he went to turn it up to what he though was normal, the scenes changed. Music exploded through the speakers loud enough to make Kristen and Julie both levitate and all of us cover our ears.

I jumped up.

Five, four, three, two, one…

POUND!...POUND!...POUND!...POUND!

I opened the door, and Amy was standing there. She was wearing brown, wide-corduroy bib overalls; a picnic-table plaid, red-and-white long-sleeved shirt; and Kermit the Frog-colored, green denim shoes with a pink poodle embroidered on each.

"Hey, nice shoes, Amy," I offered sincerely to talk about anything but the explosion of music that had no doubt shattered the silence of whatever voodoo magic she and her boxes were into that evening.

"Don't change the subject with me, Mister Chris," she said. Once again, I'm sure, quite sure, that she was thinking (insert *Wizard of Oz* Wicked Witch voice), *I'll get you and your little dog, too*!

"Sorry, it…it was an accident."

"We'll see about that. Accidents can happen once, but I've got my eye on you," she said, as she leaned about two inches from the side of my face like an intimidating prison warden. Her voice sunk lower than a pro wrestler's on steroids as she quietly said, "Oh yes…I've got my eye on you, mister."

Although I was supposed to be intimidated, I was oddly distracted by the fact that it was seven in the evening and her breath smelled distinctly of Fruit Loops.

Walking away, shaking her head, and pounding her feet hard

enough to make small rabbits and squirrels scurry for cover, she said under her breath, "Another rowdy neighbor; that's all I need."

That told me everything I wanted to know. The previous tenant had been another graduate student whom I knew well. He had completed the same internship in Oklahoma a year before I did. As a result, when I completed mine, he was graduating. We arranged that he and his wife would move out and Julie and I would move in for our last year of school. Peter was not rowdy. Peter was the anti-rowdy. His goal was to study constantly and secure a position on the faculty of the graduate school, which he did. He was no more rowdy that I am tall.

The next few months, I watched my "p's and q's" with Amy and was overly cautious to not get her bib overalls in a bundle. After all, I just wanted to get along. Besides, by now, I had learned her schedule and knew when she worked and when she was home. I could always look out the kitchen window to see if her car was there. I complied with her wishes and scheduled my time accordingly—and life was good.

One day, I had an exam. It was late fall, and the class was killing me. I was getting straight As but I was also working my proverbial rear off. I had studied for this exam for four straight days. I had been up late the night before. I had even been in a study group for it, which was rare for me. I wanted to succeed. I was as focused as a porcupine in a balloon factory. I wanted no mistakes.

I went into class, focused, and finished the exam. I was done. I knew I had done well. I didn't have my grade yet, but I had that gut feeling that I went through it like a Ginsu Knife through a Twinkie…no problem. I came home on top of the world. I was so focused on this exam that I had done something that morning that I rarely do: I got dressed and went to class without showering or shaving. I wanted every last second to study, and it worked.

Coming home, I noticed that almost all my neighbors were gone, including Amy. I screamed, "Yes!" with the same body posture and enthusiasm as Tiger Woods after winning the Masters. I could hear Martin Luther King, Jr., ringing in my ears, "Free at last! Free at last! Thank God Almighty, we are free at last!" I am not being sacrilegious. In fact, walking in, I tossed my keys on the counter, looked up at the ceiling and said out loud, "Thank you, Jesus!"

I wanted a shower, and I wanted music. I picked up my copy of Sammy Hagar's CD, *Voice of America.* (Give me a break; it was 1991.) I pushed "Power" and the "Select CD" button. Watching the CD door close was as beautiful to me as seeing a brick of gold going into a furnace to be melted and reformed. I pushed "Play" and turned the volume to a mind-decompressing 10 out of 20 so that I could hear it in the shower.

Off to the shower I went. I was in a great mood! I felt like singing, so I did (insert shower voice):

One foot on the brake and one on the gas, hey!
Well, there's too much traffic, I can't pass, no!
So I tried my best illegal move
Well, baby, black and white come and touched my groove again!
Gonna write me up a 125
Post my face wanted dead or alive
Take my license, all that jive
I can't drive 55! Oh No!
Uh!

I was doing the show. I was playing my air guitar and the works. The exam was over. "I am untouchable!" I exclaimed from the shower with a head full of shampoo. I finished up and started getting dressed to the sound of *Rock Is in My Blood.* I even took time to do an air concert for myself in front of the mirror with a hairbrush before brushing my hair. I was still in the zone when the song ended. And then it happened. In the ensuing silence, I heard the pounding of what sounded like a police raid.

POUND!...POUND!....POUND!.....POUND!......POUND!

The pounding was so hard and loud that the pictures on the wall actually shook. Just then, the cuckoo clock "coo-cooed" the hour. It was supposed to say, "Coo-Coo. Coo-Coo. Coo-Coo." However I am quite sure this time it said, *You're screwed. You're screwed. You're screwed.*

I knew it was Amy at the door. Trying to make my way down the stairs before the next song, I sprinted. Then I realized…I didn't have any pants on. Oh great, add another thing to her list to make her scream, "He's a felon! I saw him with no pants on! I'VE GONE BLIND!" I ran to the room and grabbed my pants. I ran down the hall, hopping into them, but I was too late.

"I know this guy named Richard - He's my red-necked friend - He does everything the hard way - You see, Rich don't like to bend."

I dove for the power button and pushed "Off."

POUND! POUND! POUND! POUND! POUND!

The pounds were harder and faster this time.

Looking at the cuckoo clock, I pointed and said, "You just keep your little coo-coo mouth shut, mister!"

I opened the front door and there, standing six inches from me, was Amy. She had come home from work sick. She never looked "good." However, being sick, she looked even worse. She was that grayish color of a piece of meat that's out of date. I shivered and shrugged off the visual. She was breathing so hard her bib overalls were rising and falling on her torso. Her heart was pounding so hard out of fury that she was sweating, plastering her Captain Kangaroo-like haircut to the sides of her face.

"He's a liar!" she said to the complex security guard. It was Dan, a classmate of mine who was working complex security. He was trying not to laugh with everything in him. "He told me it was an accident, last time. You're a liar!" she screamed with the same deafening, high-pitch frequency as my fifth grade teacher when she used to yell, "Fruit basket upset! You boys are just causing a fruit basket upset!"

I had visions of myself falling to the ground and covering my ears like a character from the 1950s show *The Outer Limits* as the proverbial Martian was melting his brain.

"I'm sorry. I didn't know you were home."

She was almost frothing at the mouth.

"Look, Amy, I am really, really sorry."

"You and that horrible, sinful music! You lied to me!"

"Amy, I just..."

"Liar!" she said, her voice so high it actually hurt my ears and made Dan wince. "If you hadn't come over when you moved in and told me that you would try to cooperate, I would not be so upset. But you approached me and told me so. We even tested your stereo."

"I'm sure he didn't mean it," Dan offered, looking very official in his uniform but with a not-so-hidden grin. "Look, just try to keep it down, Chris, all right?" he said almost repentantly out of due diligence while trying to hide the grin.

I knew we would both be laughing about this in class tomorrow.

"I will. Again, Amy, I am really, really sorry!"

She got close to my face, and her oversized, out-of-date, clear-plastic-rimmed glasses were actually beginning to fog up with steam. Her voice dropped to the steroid-ridden pro-wrestler level once again. "Or else," she said in a low, quiet voice.

How very odd, I thought to myself. *Her breath smells like marshmallow Easter bunnies...but it's October.* I was hearing the music from *The X-Files.* Then there was that Western standoff music again.

As she walked away, I noticed that she had little, white embroidered poodles on the sides of her hot-pink canvas tennis shoes. Dan walked away with her. He was pursing his lips to keep from laughing hysterically and losing his job. I shut the door and began to giggle. I couldn't believe it. I just couldn't believe it.

From then on, I was extra careful with the radio. Even so, Amy called complex security almost every time I turned it on. She was bored. She was quirky. She was waiting for any chance she could get, and she took advantage of every one. It got to the point that I would ask the security guards if they wanted a soda or a glass of water when they accompanied her over. It became like a friendly, mandatory visit between them and me.

I was always careful to be respectful of her. That is, all except the last week we lived there. One night, before we were about to go out for dinner, I waited until the security car went by, which meant that the guard had just started his rounds. I couldn't help it. I put in Def Leppard's *Hysteria* and let it rip. I gave it just enough time for Amy to call complex security and for them to drive over.

Then, I shut it off, right on cue. Silence.

As I walked out the door and shut it behind me, Amy was walking up with the security guard. It wasn't Dan this time. It was someone new that I didn't know.

"Hey, did you hear anyone playing loud music just now?" he asked. I could tell he felt almost forced to ask. Amy had a reputation for being a constant caller, complaining about various neighbors. As a result, he was asking strictly out of obligation.

"No, not at all," I said with a poker face.

"Just let us know if you do, okay?" he said.

I knew that he knew that it was me. I also knew that he was aware that I was moving in a week and was genuinely a nice guy. Amy also knew that he knew that it was me. She said nothing and just glared at me as she walked away.

What I learned about effective leadership from my interactions with Amy hit home the hardest the day before we moved out. I knew when Amy left for work. I knew when she left at all. She was very scheduled, very methodical, and as a result, very predictable. That day I made sure that I was outside doing something—anything really. I simply wanted to be on the back lawn when I knew that it was time for her to leave. Just like clockwork, Amy started her routine.

First she checked the kitchen shades to make sure they were down. Then, she checked the shade on the back door. Then the back light went on and off...twice. To this day, I don't know why she did it, but she always did that right before she walked out. This was the middle of the morning, and the sun was shining. Still, on and off, on and off went the light.

She opened the door, backed out, and locked it. Shut the storm door and checked it twice. Then she walked out and shut her gate. I pretended that I had to fix something on ours so that I would be smack-dab in front of her.

"Hi, Amy."

Nothing.

"Amy, can I talk to you for a minute?" I asked sincerely.

"I'm in a hurry," she responded.

"It will only take a moment, I promise, and it's kind of important."

She stopped.

"Hey, listen, I just want to talk with you for a minute, and then you never have to see me again. We're moving out tomorrow. I just have something really important to ask you."

She stood in silence and looked at me the same way the presidents of Mount Rushmore do, stone-faced and cold.

"Amy, I know that I am not the perfect neighbor. I know that my stereo and pretty much everything else about me bothers you. I just don't know why. None of the other neighbors seem to have the kind of relationship with you that you and I have.

"Honestly, you have been hostile to me since the day we met. I don't get it. I really, truly don't. I have been scratching my head trying to figure out what I did to you, and I can't come up with an answer. Can you help me here?"

"Why do you want to know?" she asked sharply and with great reservation.

"Honestly, because if I did something to offend you in any way, I want to know what it is so that I don't do it to someone else in the future. I don't want to have this kind of relationship with anyone else ever again because I really don't enjoy it." She was listening. "The second reason, Amy, is that if I knew what I did, I could at least apologize. If I apologized now, it would be empty because I wouldn't know what I was apologizing for."

She seemed to get it. She looked intently at me, not in a mean way, just in an intent way. I couldn't help but notice that she was wearing Kermit-the-Frog-green overalls with a pink shirt similar to the one worn by Piglet in *Winnie the Pooh.* She had on light-blue, canvas tennis shoes.

At least she isn't wearing the Kermit-the-Frog-green shoes with the matching overalls, I thought to myself.

She leaned forward. "I'll tell you what you did. You barged into my world. That's what you did. If I would have wanted to introduce myself, I would have. Then, when I didn't strike up a conversation, you kept pushing for me to. I didn't want to, but you wouldn't stop. I didn't think it was funny then, and I don't think it's funny now. I just wanted to be left alone, but you wouldn't do it. There, now you know."

Barged in? I thought to myself. *All I did was knock on her door.* Then it hit me. I should have listened to Julie. She has always been far more intuitive and perceptive in these matters than I am. Julie was right. All Amy wanted was to be left alone, and I didn't do it.

Amy was right, too. In my overt and outgoing manner, I did all that I could to make her laugh, smile, or even talk. I had ignored her signals and had pushed my own agenda. What a learning experience that was.

"Amy, I just want to say that I am sorry. You have taught me a lot. I can't go back and start with you again, but you have taught me a lot about interacting with others."

"Fair enough," she said, expressionless as she got into her car and left.

That was the last time I ever saw Amy. I felt a sense of closure, but even more, my mind was opened. I learned some valuable lessons about effective leadership from my interactions with Amy. I would like to share them with you so that you can learn through my experiences and mistakes.

Lesson One: Effective leaders understand that not everyone wants to interact with you. Just because you're an outgoing, fun-loving extrovert, that doesn't mean that everyone else is. It also does not mean that they should be—or have to be. Some people want to live "in their own little world." Effective leaders realize this and allow them that right. It does not make them wrong or quirky; it makes them who they are.

Lesson Two: Effective leaders do not feel that everyone must be like they are. Amy and I could not be any more different. By observing her, I came to understand that we are almost direct opposites. When I first met her, I didn't pick up on that. I tried to blow that off and look past our differences to find common ground or a similarity. The fact of the matter was that there weren't many—if any—common factors at all. Looking back, I should have let her be who she is and left her alone. Not everyone needs to be like me. I understand that now and, quite frankly, I'm glad that they are not. It makes the world a much more interesting place.

Lesson Three: Effective leaders take the input of those who are emotionally the closest to them. Julie and I are alike in countless ways. She is my best friend in the world. She is my life. However, we are also different in at least one way. She is laid-back. She will offer her opinion, and then she will leave it alone. The times that I have respected her input, I have succeeded. The times that I have ignored it, I have ended up like an armadillo on a Texas road. It just is not pretty. I have learned to seek her input and value it. A different perspective can often be a good thing.

Lesson Four: Effective leaders learn that there is a time and a place for everything. I can be as persistent as a mosquito on a humid July day when I want to be. At times, this can be good. It made me an outstanding sales professional and, even now, it often makes me a heavily booked speaker and trainer. Our daughter Kelsey gets this from me. If I express frustration when she asks me to change my mind for the seventieth time in a row, Julie comments, "Gee, where do you think she gets that from?" I usually give in to Kelsey because I love her and because she is so persistent.

Even though I have been highly successful in my professional life, I sometimes wonder if I have missed opportunities because of my constant persistence. Not everyone is going to appreciate it. Some will perceive it the way that Amy did. They just might not let me know. There is a time and place for everything. Effective leaders read their audience and react accordingly.

One final note: If your neighbor wears bib overalls, a Charlie Brown shirt, multi-colored shoes and has Captain Kangaroo hair, think before you act. He or she may not have the same outlook as you.

CHAPTER 9

EVERYONE SHOULD MEET LAURI

FIVE TRUTHS THAT BUILD RELATIONSHIPS

As we have studied personal excellence, we have sought to understand and appreciate the common factors that exist among people who live with vitality and passion. We have asked ourselves: What do these individuals understand or grasp that empowers them to live such vibrant lives and experience joys and successes that many others only dream of?

One thing that we've learned is: Don't become jealous of people who are successful. Instead, *learn from them.* This is the difference between continuing on a journey of personal excellence and becoming stagnant. We all know people that others just love to hate. They are too pretty or are too handsome. They have the right job and the best clothes. They are the happy people who sing to the muzak in the elevator. What if you looked instead at these people with a learning mind, open to opportunity?

Ask yourself what the individuals that you want to be like have in common. What themes or dynamics do they include in their life and their way of thinking that you can learn from and use in your own life? Does feeling certain ways empower them to accomplish what they do? Have they mastered certain interactions that strengthen their self-confidence and their relationships with others? Have they somehow managed to meet their internal needs in a way that eliminates self-doubt?

Over the years, we have asked ourselves these same questions in observing individuals that we admire. These individuals had reached a level of personal excellence in their lives that we wanted to reach. In an effort to understand what they had mastered that we, too, wanted to master, we began to study them. In the process, we discovered five common themes that consistently surface in connection with these individuals *and continue to fuel their fire for life.* These individuals understand these five principles first as related to themselves and then as related to others. We can represent these concepts with the acronym LAURI, where each letter represents one of the concepts:

They feel **L**oved, therefore they are loving towards others.
They feel **A**ccepted, therefore they are accepting of others.
They feel **U**nderstood, therefore they seek to understand others.
They feel **R**espected, therefore they respect others.
They feel **I**ncluded, therefore they include others.

Most of us know from childhood what it's like to be picked last for a team or to be misunderstood on the teenage dating scene. Those feelings don't go away when we become adults. We generally just talk about them less and try to ignore them.

We do not outgrow the need to be loved, accepted, understood, respected, and included. If you aren't convinced, we can convince you easily. Just watch a staff meeting and notice how early some coworkers arrive to sit next to the boss. Watch how they react when they don't feel loved, accepted, understood, respected, or included, or any combination of these.

Our families, coworkers, and clients all need to have their needs met. Clients want to be respected, understood, and included in a good business deal. Family members also want to be loved, accepted, understood, respected, and included. In fact, most family problems occur when one or more of these areas are not being met. Ask yourself how this list applies to you. What can you do for your family so their needs are met?

But first, ask yourself if you take time to feel love toward yourself. Do you accept yourself, faults and all? Do you seek to understand yourself and what drives you? Do you treat yourself with respect? Do you include yourself among your priorities and in your busy schedule?

In every case we studied, we realized that these individuals led lives of personal excellence because they understood the incredible power of these five concepts. Each one accepted who he or she was, regardless of height, weight, skin color, hair color, physical or intellectual abilities or disabilities. Each understood his or her strengths and unique and special presence in this world. Each had respect for himself or herself as a spiritual, emotional, and physical entity, and treated himself or herself in a way that reflected and embraced that respect. Finally, each made himself or herself feel included in life by being with positive people and experiences, and giving themselves permission to celebrate life.

Now that we know the five dynamics that they applied to their lives, let's see how we can apply those dynamics to our own lives. If we look at how we apply each of these, we will more fully understand the unique and wonderful relationship each of us can have with ourselves. This will shape and change everything that we do because we will go from living for pure outcome to living with purpose. We will talk about purpose later in this book, but let's lay the foundation by understanding these five principles, so that we also can lay a foundation for amazing progress in each of our lives.

Each person developed a LOVE for who they are. We are not saying that they developed arrogance or conceit. We are not talking about the confidence of someone who drives a black 1979 Pontiac Trans Am with a T-top while wearing a partially unbuttoned gold shirt, with three gold necklaces dangling below Elvis-style hair and mirrored sunglasses pulled down just far enough to wink at you. That is just wrong for so many reasons.

No, the men and women we studied, from young to old, loved themselves as special contributors to life. They looked for the good in themselves, and they found it. They looked for the inner beauty that they possess and the strength that comes from within.

They were people who said to themselves, "I am special. I matter. I have value, and I can make a difference in this world!" Then, they lived out these concepts. They saw each day as a gift.

Even more, they saw themselves as gifts. Again, they did not do this in an arrogant or conceited way. They did this in a way that empowered them to engage with others who would love them for who they were, and who treated and valued them as someone special who matters and can make a difference.

"Arrogant" or "conceited" describes someone who thinks he or she is better than everyone else and keeps pointing that out. *Confidence is when you believe in yourself and know what you are capable of.*

How about you? Do you see yourself as someone who matters, is special, and can make a difference? If you don't, that's probably because someone else made you feel negative about yourself. Someone may have described you negatively, and you decided to carry that around with you. You decided to believe it and own it. If that is the case, go back, revisit the "what is in your glass" concept, and ask yourself why someone would have done that. I think you will find that they needed to build themselves up by putting you down.

If they said you looked silly, ask yourself why. If you were a college student dressed in a chicken outfit and standing on a corner passing out coupons for the Chicken Shack, there may be some validity to the comment. (Ah yes, college memories!) If they called you the human chicken without malice, you could laugh along. It's different if they put you down for some other reason.

Separate temporary negative comments from the permanent you. Comments do not reflect you; they're just someone else's self-perception projected onto you. (If they're in a chicken suit and saying you look silly, I think they are in denial.) Love yourself for who you are. Be yourself. *Look for and find the good and positive in your personality every day. Look for and find the good and positive in your gift of intellect every day.*

Do not compare yourself to someone else. You'll always fall short if you compare yourself with someone smarter, wiser, or perceived to be better looking or better at something else. If you constantly compare yourself to those who are not as smart, not as wise, or not perceived to be as good looking or as good at something as you, you may be covering up your own feelings of inadequacy. *Look within yourself to find the good in you.* Find the strengths. Find the talents. Find the beauty. When you do, I guarantee that suddenly other perceived flaws or shortcomings will be greatly diminished or become unimportant.

Love yourself for who you are. Remind yourself daily of that. Go back to the affirmations that we spoke of. Take ownership of them. The people we have studied all developed a love for themselves and an appreciation for who they are. You can do the same thing!

Each person ACCEPTED themselves, perceived shortcomings and all. This is powerful. *Accept yourself for who you are.* If you are going to be *accepting of others,* you must first *accept yourself.* If you are going to be *accepted by others,* you much first *accept yourself.* Accepting who you are means embracing your special nature.

I still remember a great example of this. Her name is Betsy. I met her in 1993 when we lived in Pryor Creek, Oklahoma. She had a tremendous amount of confidence. She was in her late fifties and about forty pounds overweight, or maybe more. When she smiled, she had a big gap where a tooth used to be, and she had ears about the size of a jackrabbit's. Even so, she was genuinely happy and just a hoot to be around.

She loved who she was and accepted herself, so jackrabbit ears and a missing tooth made no difference. She accepted herself, and it showed because she accepted everyone else, too. She was not resentful of anyone who was perceived to be prettier or had smaller ears.

I don't know if you have super-human ears or a missing tooth, but whoever you are, accept yourself for who you are. You don't need to be anything but yourself. If you are short, accept yourself. (At least that is what the voices in my head keep telling me.) If you are tall, accept yourself. If you are overweight or underweight, accept yourself. Whoever you are, however you are, accept yourself.

If your doctor tells you that you need to lose weight to be healthy, do not smugly say, "Well, the Irelans think I'm just fine the way I am." By accepting who you are, you will gain the power to change something that may need to be changed. Maybe you do need to lose weight to be healthier; maybe you need to quit smoking, drink less alcohol, start exercising, read more books, or watch less garbage on TV.

If you need to make any of these or other changes, repeat this phrase, *I accept me for who I am, and I have the power to change anything about me that I want to.* This doesn't mean you can make yourself taller. But you have to power to make any lifestyle change, once you accept you and the power within you. Each of us has power within us. Each of us has drive. Awaken that incredible power by accepting yourself for who you are!

Each person UNDERSTOOD themselves, including their strengths and weaknesses. Each of the people we studied had sought to understand what drove themselves as part of their journey of personal excellence. This gave them confidence and the ability to take an honest look at their strengths and weaknesses. The power behind this is amazing! Once you understand yourself, you can make the most of your strengths. When you do this, you are able to better find your place in the world, in relationships, and in life.

To truly understand yourself, you must first love and accept yourself. Then you'll find yourself much easier to understand. You'll be able to understand others much more as well. If we understand our strengths, we can learn to focus our time and energy on them. That certainly does not mean that we should deny or ignore our weaknesses. Just the opposite is true. Understanding our weaknesses empowers us to embrace them. Why would you want to embrace a weakness? The reason is simple. *You want to embrace a weakness so that you master it instead of it mastering you.*

For example, you understand that you have a weakness for details. Embracing this empowers you to seek the assistance and input of others who are strong in that area. If you have a weakness for junk food, cigarettes, alcohol, or anything else that should be done in moderation or not at all, start by embracing this reality and become empowered to take steps to keep from falling prey to that weakness. Once you accept your strengths and weaknesses with an honest mind, you can more fully balance life, engage with others, and become the complementary strength to someone else's weakness.

Do you understand your strengths and weaknesses? We're not asking you to rent a billboard to shout out your weaknesses. You can find therapy for those inclinations. But the way to tackle an area of weakness is to start by taking a good look at it. Often our weaknesses can be substitutions for something else. A weakness for junk food or alcohol can be a hiding place to escape from dealing with life or our place in it. When we don't know how to deal with situations, circumstances, or relationships, we may turn to these hiding places.

Knowing our weaknesses allows us to deal with them. If someone turns to excessive food, drugs, or alcohol to avoid life, their true weakness is non-acceptance of themselves. Those who begin to truly accept and love themselves will *understand* themselves and not need these escape hatches. Do you seek to understand yourself enough to know your weaknesses and begin to deal with them? If so, ask yourself what your weaknesses are and become empowered to deal with them. Seek to understand your strengths and weaknesses better, and watch a new journey of personal excellence unfold!

Each person RESPECTED themselves. Once you understand the power of self-respect, you can see clearly who respects themselves and who does not. If they do not love themselves, accept themselves, or understand themselves, why would they have respect for themselves? The individuals that we observed acted in a manner that showed they respected themselves.

Respect means "to esteem" or "place a value on." These individuals held esteem for themselves and placed significant value on themselves as physical, emotional, spiritual, and intellectual beings. They treated themselves like something valuable. They treated themselves like an investment. This was reflected in their behavior, their associations, and their actions. They took better care of themselves. They committed to maintaining their spiritual, emotional, and physical health. They avoided relationships and interactions that were abusive, offensive, or belittling. They would not accept negative treatment, like being put down by others.

I remember a consulting relationship that I had with a placement firm. The owner had asked me to help his employees understand themselves and their clients better so that the business would grow. What I found was a sad picture. The owner put down his staff, saying things such as, "When you can operate at my level…" or, "When you get as good at this as I am…" or, "You will never be as great as I am at that…" How sad. He had surrounded himself with people with no self-respect. They felt that they could not function in any worthwhile way without him. They felt they needed to draw from his power, talent, and ability because he reinforced this daily.

When I started the consult, I asked him not to address me as he addressed his employees—and he ignored me. As they say in our daughter's second-grade class, he needed to turn his listening ears on. The second time he did this to me, I was reminded of our children's kindergarten teacher, Mary Halter, from a few years ago. She would say, "I told you once. I told you twice. Next time I won't be so nice." She used this message to gently encourage the children to stop their inappropriate behavior. My consulting client could have used that kindergarten advice when he was forty-six.

One day I announced that I was terminating our business relationship. I was kind, professional, open, and honest. I did not address how he treated his staff because I knew he would not hear what I was saying. He didn't see that he himself was keeping his business from growing.

I simply informed him that I had far too much respect for myself to be around that type of behavior even one more day. I refused to let him speak to me in such a way. Some people only hear what they want to hear and will not look at their own weaknesses. Pointing the finger and blaming those around them is much easier. Obviously, this was a lifestyle he was not going to change. He reminded me of the captain going down with the ship while lifejackets were floating all around him.

As you think about this example, don't focus on the business owner's actions, but on mine. I left the professional relationship because I have enough self-respect to terminate destructive interactions with others. What happened to him? You guessed it. Within a few months, he was no longer in business, still angry at his employees and believing they were to blame.

What about you? Do you place high esteem on who you are? Do you find worth in the value that you have as a special, wonderful, and unique person? Are you filling your glass daily with words from others that build you up, make you more confident, fuel your love for yourself, add to your acceptance of yourself, and help you better understand your strengths?

If not, now is the time for action! Far too often we have seen women (men, too, but usually women), anywhere from fifteen to seventy-five years old, who are in relationships where they are not respected. They remain in these relationships when they should not. They don't respect themselves, and neither does the person physically or verbally putting them down. Sometimes you may not seem to be respecting yourself when you're trying to accomplish long-term goals. (It got pretty hot inside that chicken suit, let me tell you!) But that's not the same as surrounding yourself personally and professionally with people who tear you down instead of building you up. That's not acceptable once you develop true self-respect. Begin this portion of your journey of self-respect by answering the following questions:

What gives me value?

This comes from within, not from without. Others do not give you value. They can only appreciate the value that you embody. Let me repeat that. You do not get your value personally or professionally from others. You can only share the beauty and value that exists within you, and they can appreciate it.

How will I show myself respect today?

Do something for yourself that will give you a physical reminder of your self-respect. Remind yourself why you are doing it and tell yourself that you matter, you are special, and you can make a difference. It can be something big or small. It can be anything that benefits you and reminds you to respect yourself for who you are. You truly are special!

Each person INCLUDED themselves in the celebration of life. People often give so much of themselves in helping others enjoy life that they forget to celebrate it themselves. Take time to celebrate! Each of the people we observed did something that they enjoyed, and it fueled their passion for life. Two groups of people often forget to include themselves in the celebration of life—women, who are givers or nurturers by nature, and male and female caregivers. These nurturers get so absorbed in giving that they forget to receive or feel guilty when they do. Julie and I are giving you a permission slip to take recess or a field trip each day.

Do something for you. Do something silly and fun. Reward yourself with a cup of gourmet coffee. Go for a walk. Read a book. Give a copy of this book to a friend and be the one "in the know." Take time for a hobby. Visit with a friend to enjoy their company. Buy a pogo stick, but use it on the back patio because if you pogo on the driveway, the neighbors may begin to talk. If you are going to be that silly, you might as well pogo in a chicken suit! Hey, don't laugh; I've seen strange things when people start to celebrate life. The point is this: Include yourself in the celebration, and you will feel energized, revitalized, and refreshed.

Take the time to get to know **LAURI**. Ask yourself if you treat yourself with love and acceptance. Do you seek to understand both your strengths and weaknesses to act upon them? Are you surrounding yourself with people who are positive toward you and avoiding or discontinuing relationships where they are not? Do you include yourself in the celebration of life?

When you've implemented these five dynamics into your thoughts, actions, and way of life, your journey of personal excellence is well under way! Take time daily to give yourself positive affirmations. Say them out loud, write them down, review them, or do all three. The sooner you own these dynamics as your own, the sooner you will experience the empowering miracle of you. As we close this chapter, I just want to remind you, if you are going to celebrate by buying a pogo stick and a chicken suit, use discretion when you pogo.

Chapter 10

When In Albania, Do As The Albanians

To Be An Effective Leader, Try To Relate To Everyone In Some Way

Leading by design means leading by intention. To do that, we have to understand that we are the leader—whether we choose to be or not, and whether we are aware of this or not. When we understand the scope of our leadership and its impact and implications at any given time, we begin to think much more deliberately about our actions. We also begin to act much more intentionally for better outcomes.

This had an incredible impact on me in 1999. Two different examples come to mind. The first took place in June of that year. Julie and I had traveled to Albania as ambassadors for adoption on behalf of our adoption agency in Washington, D.C. As representatives, we were helping to increase relations with the country of Albania and with the orphanage from which we would adopt our son Connor one month later.

We knew we were serving as leaders during the trip. If all went well, we would be allowed to bring our son home, along with two other families adopting children from the orphanage. In other words, we needed to be very aware of the fact that we were leaders and had a responsibility. We represented the people of the United States to leaders in Albania's legal system. We represented a freedom, a hope, and a completely different way of life for those children. We offered opportunity and progress.

During our trip to build bridges and strengthen relations, we attended a banquet for leaders of the Albanian legal system. We did our best to work through the interpreter to overcome language barriers and connect in the best possible way. To show our openness and willingness to embrace Albanian culture, society, and history, we did all that we could to observe the country's customs and traditions. I vividly recall one ritual that is significant to people of that part of Albania.

We were going to share a toast during the meal, and the men offered to share their homemade drink, a strong whiskey-like beverage, with me. Recognizing our leadership role, Julie encouraged me to take part each time they invited us to participate in something like this. We did not do it to be patronizing; we sincerely appreciated their culture and traditions. Desiring to stay the course and keeping our leadership in mind, I joined them at their invitation to share the drink.

Keep two things in mind. First, there is a big difference between ordering a beverage that you are familiar with and know you will enjoy vs. consuming a random beverage and not knowing what to expect. Second, there is a great time difference between America and Albania, which are on opposite sides of the world. We were only there for three days, so we had little time to adjust to the roughly eleven-hour time difference. The evening banquet was taking place at about the same time as an early morning breakfast in America. My jetlag had not worn off, and I was out of my time zone and my routine. Still, as they say, "When in Rome…" In this case, it was, "When in Albania..."

As they handed me my glass, I thought, *Okay, you're Irish; how bad could this be?* I held it to my lips and began to drink alongside my Albanian banquet guests. My contacts began to dry up as if they had been left out overnight. I have no proof, but I am sure that a combination of smoke and steam came from my ears like that of Grandpa Munster from *The Munsters* television show of the 1960s. I could picture Herman Munster jumping up and down, laughing and waving his arms as he saw the smoke come from my ears.

My lips went from being on fire to being numb. If I had spoken, I would have sounded like an incomprehensible person leaving a four-hour dental appointment. I could not prove it, but I was sure that my tongue was on fire. For the first time in my life, I felt every millimeter of my throat, esophagus, and stomach. I could tell you with precise accuracy exactly when the liquid hit each area. If I had hiccupped, I was sure I would have shot flames. I could feel the roots of my hair on the top of my head as every inch of me began to react and perspire. This was quite the experience.

You are a leader, I told myself as I held the glass up and smiled as if to say, *This is great stuff!* In my mind, I was thinking, *Is my life insurance paid?*

I dare not take a glass of water; that would be insulting, I thought to myself. I have always admired Texans for being able to eat extraordinarily hot foods. Now, however, I pictured myself standing in a dusty Texas street in an old ghost town, caught in a duel of hot sauces. In my mind, I was staring my Texas competitor square in the eyes as I said, "Bring it on, Texas tough guy." I pictured drinking the hottest sauce they had and then looking to the sky, laughing demonically, and saying, "That's all you have, cowboy?"

I am pathetic, I thought to myself. *Get a grip*. But I continued to visualize the Texas hot sauce showdown. *I can take anything*, I thought to myself. Looking over at my imaginary Texas competitor, I thought to myself, *Let's see how tough you really are.* More Western standoff music began to play as I poured my imaginary Texas friend a glass of this Albanian beverage. I pictured watching as he drank it and his hat blew straight off his head. I pictured ducking as he breathed fire over my head. I felt proud.

As I pictured this, I sat burning and sweating, and I think the word, "Mommy?" stumbled across my numb lips in child-like desperation. We were told that the beverage had been made by hand in one of their basements. I had visions of books I had read about Prohibition and how some people went blind by not making liquor the correct way. I must have done okay, though.

One of the Albanians took off his tie and gave it to me as a gift for being a real man.

I lived through the experience and clearly can laugh about it now. My point is that I was there in a leadership role and I needed to act like a leader. I had to be aware that any self-serving activity could diminish my leadership abilities. By taking part in this cultural ritual without experiencing spontaneous internal combustion, I was able to fulfill my leadership role. This (combined with many and much more significant actions and interactions by Julie and the others) accomplished our objective. We not only brought our son home, but we opened the way for countless other children to experience a land of plenty and homes of opportunity.

I never lost sight of why we were there. I thought of those to whom this was important and life changing. When I did this, my one small comedic task did not seem overwhelming at all. The responsibility of realizing that I was a leader, though, had a tremendous impact.

The second example took place during November of that same year. Due to international adoption laws at that time, we could not take Connor to China with us to pick up his sister Kelsey. International adoption at that time was a one-way ticket into America until a child became a citizen. Connor had only been in America for a month before we left for China. Because of this, Julie's parents enjoyed time with their new grandson. Julie and I played a similar role in China to the one that we had in Albania. We were leaders for our adoption agency, working to strengthen relations with the Chinese government and particularly to strengthen American adoption ties.

This example also involved a gastronomical experience. We had asked our translator to show us where local people eat, rather than tourist restaurants. We went to a nice restaurant in an upscale part of town. Because the economy in China was very different than that of the United States, we could visit some of the nicer restaurants for a quite reasonable budget. As our translator guided us to the restaurant, I quickly realized that I was "not in Kansas anymore." Those of you who have been to China may be expecting what I am going to describe next. I, however, was not.

I am accustomed to America where you are handed a menu with descriptions of food selections creatively written to tell how each one will be prepared. In many nicer restaurants, the wait staff lists the specials and actually describes how each is prepared. They create mental pictures to give you the best opportunity to select among the options offered. The descriptions are often so accurate that you can almost smell and taste the food, particularly if you are hungry. The wonderful culture of China brings a whole new meaning to this process.

As we walked into the restaurant, I was suddenly reminded of the feed mill in Elm Grove, Wisconsin, where I worked during high school. The mill had a garden store attached to the front that offered plants and gardening tools, water softener salts, and pet supplies. This included the pets. The store had a wide variety of small pets ranging from hamsters and gerbils to spiders, snakes, fish, turtles, and other living things that people keep as pets. You could not miss them. The cages and aquatic tanks were prominently displayed up and down the aisles as you walked in.

The restaurant in China was much the same. There were cages filled with turtles, snakes, spiders, and various other small aquatic and non-aquatic living things. The reality was that this was our menu. I suddenly went from being quite hungry to feeling a complete absence of hunger. Nothing was wrong or out of place about this. I simply was not accustomed to it and was once again feeling jetlag on the other side of the world. This was the equivalent of an early morning meal for us again, but it wasn't like getting bacon and eggs from the refrigerator. Fundamentally, there is no difference. A pig and a chicken in cages should be the same as bacon and eggs in a refrigerator. Still, it was not anything that I had experienced before.

As we were guided to our seats, we walked by the cages. I

think one of the animals gestured to me in the same fashion as an upset Chicago driver, seeming to say, "Don't pick me, or else!" *You can do this,* I assured to myself. *You are a leader, here for more than just your own interests.*

We were greeted and ordered our drinks as the waitress described our selections. Our translator took time to explain everything with the utmost care. I felt ill. Julie sensed this and suggested that I order anything that resembled something we would have in the United States.

"Fish!" I accidentally said out loud. "The fish sounds wonderful!"

"Smart choice," Julie assured me, while ordering something that she could not get America.

I ordered the fish and blocked the other options from my mind completely. It is amazing what the power of concentration can do. It is also amazing how you can do this when you realize that you are a leader and that others are watching you, consciously or unconsciously.

Think about your own life. Are there times when you are called to be an intentional leader? Sometimes it happens quite expectedly. Other times, it is quite by surprise. For example, in that restaurant in China, some people offered to pay Julie money if they could have a cut piece of her long blond hair. She politely refused but was gracious as she addressed them.

Your leadership might not involve funny experiences in restaurants. It might be something entirely different, such as admitting a mistake or standing up for what is right. It might even be acting with intentional leadership even though no one is watching you. One of my favorite phrases about acting as a leader when you are being watched—and when you are not—can be found in the women's varsity basketball locker room at Concordia University Wisconsin. As the young ladies suit up and exit the locker room, they walk through the doorway and pass under a phrase that says, "Integrity: It's what you do when no one is looking."

While spectators watch these young women play against other teams, they see them as leaders on the court, but they are also leaders at other times. They are leaders when they practice as a team with no crowd watching. They are leaders when they practice a particular shot by themselves in an empty gym. They are leaders when they are off the court but others know that they represent that team and that school. That phrase above the doorway reminds them that they are leaders all the time.

The same holds true for each of us. We are leaders. We represent more than just ourselves. We represent the group, family, company, association, or school that we are part of or connected to. At the heart of deliberate and designed leadership is doing the right thing, both when we know we are being watched and when we do not. Doing the right thing for the sake of doing the right thing is truly leading by design.

We will never know the number of lives that we have touched and the number of people who have been influenced by our leadership. We do know, however, that our leadership can and does make a difference in this world. Our leadership is noticed. Our leadership inspires others to be leaders as well. In doing so, we affect far more than simply the situation at hand and the people involved right now in our actions.

We may never really know the strength and ultimate outcome of our leadership, but we do know this: Leadership carried out by design, rather than by default, never returns empty. Leadership by design can bring a team, an army, or even an entire nation to a new place or progress. It all starts with one person who decides to take action, one person who wants to make a difference and experience the joy of that decision and that action.

Leadership does not have to be complicated. It may be as easy as focusing on the good in ourselves, in others, in our situation, and in life. When you focus on what you can control, you are in control. Effective leaders have focused historically on what they can control and have led others to focus on these things as well.

Achieving personal excellence means that each of us needs to do the same thing. When we do, we realize that we don't need to over-think personal excellence or effective leadership. By focusing on a few simple things that we can control, we can make significant progress on our journey of excellence. Individuals who become star leaders do this regularly and consistently. As they do, their level of effectiveness continues to increase, and so do their personal joy and professional satisfaction. No one wakes up and says, "I will change my whole life today." Even if they did, they would soon fall back into old habits. Small changes each day and each week make a world of difference over the long-term.

Now that we've examined the key points of making progress on our journey of personal excellence and have begun to examine how that builds into leadership, let's take a closer look at what effective leadership means. What is a leader? A leader is someone who others follow. That sounds simple and, in fact, it is. A leader sets the way, charts the course, or paves the path for others to achieve similar results. A leader is followed, looked up to, or copied to some degree. In short, a leader brings someone with them on a journey. This is done by keeping in mind the five key truths from our last chapter. Leaders remember that everyone wants to be love, accepted, understood, respected, and included.

As we take this journey of personal excellence, it's important to realize that each of us is a leader on some level. You may be thinking, "I'm not a leader." You may be thinking, "I don't have an executive office or management title," or, "I'm not responsible for managing anyone," or, "I haven't been promoted recently, and I don't own a company."

While these statements may be true at face value, you are a leader in some capacity. Each of us is—whether janitor or CEO. The sooner we examine and accept that truth, the sooner we can begin to take ownership of leadership in our lives. Here is a problem many organizations overlook. Most companies train only the "higher-ups." But the lower that people are on the training scale, the more "face time" they usually have with clients and customers.

Here is an example: You are in building for the first time, and you are lost. You may see the janitor and ask how to get where you are going. Your first interaction with that business lies in the hands of someone pushing a broom. What is that person's attitude like? First impressions of a company are created before the client walks in the door. Whenever we go to meet with a new client, we look for the janitor and ask questions. We want to learn what his or her attitude is. This informs and empowers us, allowing us to learn something about our clients through what some of their employees are like.

Most leaders' attitudes are passed down from employee to employee. This is somewhat like the game "Telephone" that little girls like to play while sitting in a circle. One girl thinks up a silly phrase and whispers it to the next giggly little girl. She whispers it to the next, and so on. The outcome is not even close to the original phrase.

This same thing takes place in companies and groups everywhere. In these settings, however, it is not a game. Written communication is the key to ending this game. But we still find the strength of management's communication skills and attitude reflected in the janitor pushing the broom or the mailroom employee running around the building. Why? Although the words may be different among different areas of companies, the attitudes passed down from upper management, or passed from one department to the next, continue to be passed on through the employees. Each person in the company is a leader, regardless of their title.

Leaders become leaders in one of two ways—either by design or by default. It is that simple. Individuals who don't understand or realize that they are leaders usually are leaders *by default.* They don't lead because of anything that they consciously did or intended. Others started following them, and they were not even aware of it. Have you ever been in a situation or a company where one person is always asked for input, even though their title doesn't indicate that they can give such advice? They may be the person to ask while the true job title rests on someone else's shoulders. Whether we are aware that other people follow us or not, our actions are being watched and our leadership is setting an example, bad or good.

The danger of leading by default is that we aren't aware of being watched or setting the tone for others. When this happens, we don't conduct ourselves or plan our words and actions with this in mind. We may make mistakes or show poor judgment by focusing on the immediate outcome or being driven by emotion. Those who follow us can't read our minds, so they may not understand the reasons behind our actions. They may copy these actions without understanding why or the possible positive or negative outcomes.

This became evident to me following my 1987 car accident. I was told that my chances of walking were slim to none. I had a choice that I quickly realized would affect not only Julie, my friends, and me, but also everyone who looked to me as a leader. I was about to turn 21. For several years, I had been president, founder, or in another leadership role in basically every organization or group that I had been associated with. Many individuals looked up to me. Many of them counted on my direction, guidance, and input to help them be successful. I was aware that I was a leader, and I was always, and to this day remain, pleased to do so.

Following the car accident, I found myself in a different leadership capacity than before. As I began the long and uncertain road to recovery with determination and boundless enthusiasm, I found myself being watched by others. This happened up close and from a distance. I learned the full impact after I regained my ability to walk and returned to college to complete my undergraduate studies. I was humbled and almost moved to tears by some of the comments that I heard.

I remember a conversation between two members of our

college football team. I was walking to class, passing the athletic training room not too long after I had been released from the hospital. As I passed the room where Jack and Tim were talking, I overheard their conversation. They were completely unaware that I was there.

"Jack," said Tim, "that injury looks serious. I doubt that you will be able to play in the game next week."

"Oh, I'll play, Tim. I will play, believe me," Jack said with complete confidence. "It's just a matter of setting my mind to it."

"I don't know," said Tim, his voice filled with a healthy dose of skepticism. "Guys with an injury like that are usually laid up for a few weeks."

"That's because they choose to be," said Jack with a confident and kind, yet authoritative tone.

"They choose to be?" asked Tim, quite intrigued by this statement.

"Yes, if there is one thing that I learned from Chris Irelan's broken back, it's that determination can make a huge difference in your recovery. In fact, seeing Chris return to school, I am convinced that your attitude can change your outcome."

"You have a point," Tim agreed. "I can't believe that he's actually walking again and back in school already. I heard that his chances of walking were slim to none."

"That's exactly what I'm talking about! It was mind over body. That guy is a real leader, whether he realizes it or not. When I think of his broken back and I look at my injury, which is nothing more than a pulled muscle, I realize that I can do this. I can play next week. It's just a matter of mind over body, that's all. I admire his determination. He wouldn't take no for an answer, not even from himself. Personally, that's the way I want to live my life, and that's why I'm telling you that I will be playing in next week's game."

As I heard this, I felt humbled and proud at the same time. I was moved. I had not determined to walk again to be a leader. It was simply something that I had to do for Julie and for me. I heard this conversation by accident as I was walking down the hall. Yet, in some simple way in the continuum of life, I knew that I was meant to hear it.

My acts of self-determination, done primarily for my own self-interests, had set an example for my peers. It became evident in the weeks to come that this was one of many dialogues taking place among my fellow students and professors. Individuals who chose not to settle for average, and who wanted the best for themselves and the people that mattered to them, used my determination as an example for their own lives. I had not thought of myself as a leader until I heard the conversation between Jack and Tim, but it was the first of many that I would hear or be told about.

The next week, I attended the football game and wanted to see if Jack would play. As the second quarter started, I watched him put on his helmet and hit the field. I was humbled, but I was also inspired. If this single situation in my life, a simple but serious injury, could allow me to be this much of an example and a leader, what else was I capable of?

What else were others capable of that they were not yet aware of? If I had been this much of an effective leader by *default*, what type of leadership was I capable of if I chose to be a leader by *design*? What else was Jack capable of? What is each of us capable of doing in our lives that we are not doing now? Even more so, what type of intentional and effective leadership is each of us capable of if we set our minds to it and act with design and determination?

That was a positive situation where I led by default. I did not intend to have a positive impact on Jack or anyone else; I simply was determined to take charge of my future and be able to walk again. Unfortunately, leading by default often has a negative outcome as we focus on outcome, instead of our impact and influence on others. In my case, the result happened to be positive. Usually leading by default is not.

A great example of leading by default can be seen in parenting. Sometimes, as parents, we break the rules accidentally or on purpose. We may tell a white lie, which we know that we should not do, out of self-interest or to avoid an awkward situation. If we are parents, we remember that little eyes are always watching us and little ears are always listening to us. If we have led by default, just as we are about to discipline our child, we may stop when we hear them say something or see them do something that they should not have said or done. When we look into their little eyes, we see mirror reflections of ourselves and hear words that we said not long ago or see something we did not long ago.

If you are a parent, you probably have been there. We were so focused on achieving an outcome or expressing an emotion that we temporarily forgot we are leaders who are being watched and copied. Needless to say, these lessons, especially with our children, remind us to be aware that we are leaders. As such, we should be intentional in our thought and have design in our communication. But enough discussing leading by default, let's focus on leading by design.

As you finish this chapter on leading by design, apply it to your own life. You may not have had to drink rotgut liquor in Albania. You may not have had your back broken. But if you take a moment to think about examples in your own life, you most likely will see times when you led by default and by design.

When I recovered from my broken back, I was leading by default. Thankfully, I was leading in a good way. Years later when I was at the banquet in Albania, I was leading by design. Again, thankfully, I was leading in a good way. If each of us focuses on leading by design, we will lead much more consistently and have many more positive outcomes. Make the choice today to lead more consistently by design, and watch your leadership flourish!

Chapter 11

Elvis Has Left The Building

Learn To Inspire vs. Motivate

In the mid- to late 1970s, some thirty years before this book was written, motivational speakers began to appear in corporate America at annual conventions, corporate outings, and retreats. During the early and mid-1980s, this phenomenon reached its peak. Motivational speakers were everywhere. Not to diminish their talent or ability, but they became "a dime a dozen." There were so many that if one wasn't available, you simply went on to the next one.

As this trend continued in the 1980s, several prominent motivational speakers began to be more in demand, become booked more often, and demand higher fees. Not long after that, corporate America jumped on the bandwagon as well. Soon, executives—from presidents to vice presidents to middle management—were giving pep talks to their employees. They arrived with a great deal of energy and enthusiasm. They said things that were funny or told an inspiring story. They evoked laughter and other emotions. The meeting room would be filled with excitement.

In some instances at the peak of this phenomenon, beach balls were even thrown around the room or confetti-type material fell from the ceiling. Some presentations included loud music, and participants were encouraged to clap loudly or dance. This was a sign of what the speaking industry was going through in the 1980s and how it affected management in corporate America.

The challenge with this type of motivation is that it has no lasting effect. Try going back even a short time after the event and asking the participants to repeat the speaker's main point. In many cases, they can't. They can list one or two memorable or entertaining stories, but they can't give details about the substance of the presentation.

Further, if you ask them about the take-home value they derived, you rarely hear anything of substance or value. This is not to criticize the motivational speaking industry of the '80s—or even today. It's simply an objective observation of what took place, what was achieved, and (more importantly) the opportunities that were missed.

In the 1990s, I became friends with Wayne, the retired CEO of a Fortune 500 company. Since Julie and I were studying those who pursued personal excellence and were effective leaders, I had a conversation with Wayne about that.

"You know, Chris," he said. "I can remember back in the late 1970s and 1980s. I was manager, vice president, and then president of a company. It was a very 'in' thing to have a motivational speaker at the annual conference."

"Tell me about that," I said. "I want to know what the experience was like."

"The experience was just that—an experience," Wayne said. "I wouldn't call it an education process or a group dynamic; it was an experience."

"What do you mean by an experience?" I asked.

"There was a lot of hype," he said. "The speaker would start with an elaborate introduction, listing all of his or her credentials and many accomplishments. More significantly, they would list the key people of influence that they had the opportunity to speak to or share the stage with. It was a lot of hype. I am not saying it was bad; it was just a lot of hype. It got your attention for the moment, if nothing else. Usually, there *was* nothing else."

"What else was it like?" I asked.

"There always was introductory music," he said. "You felt like you were waiting for Elvis Presley to come on stage. Then when the speaker did come on stage, there was a lot of clapping and cheering. Funny thing was, we didn't know why we were clapping or cheering for this person, other than the fact that someone was told to lead the group in doing it—usually me as the executive—and so we always did. Like I said, it was a lot of hype."

"What else can you tell me about the experience?" I asked.

"The speakers really knew how to move people's emotions. Some were better than others. We tried to do as much homework as we could before we brought speakers in," he said. "And the really good ones knew how to work the crowd."

"Begging the question," I said, "what do you mean by 'working the crowd?'"

"Well," he said with a smile, "as someone who has spoken to many people and given addresses to other companies throughout the country, I've learned a thing or two about speaking. And these individuals played one particular angle."

"What was that?" I asked.

"They tried to get at the heart of the audience's emotions. In other words, as I watched and observed these brilliant speakers through the years, I noticed that they could get people to laugh or to nearly cry. And right when people felt the heat of that emotion, the speaker would switch gears willingly in another direction. If the speakers were really good, they had people on the edge of their seats."

"That sounds very entertaining," I said, quite honestly.

"It was," he replied. "As I said, it was like going to an Elvis Presley concert."

As we write this book and I recall this story, I must admit that I knew exactly what he was talking about. My half-siblings are quite a bit older than me, so when Elvis Presley came to Milwaukee, at the height of his popularity, for a concert in the early 1970s, I was a small boy, probably no older than six years old. My teen-age half-brothers and sisters owned nearly all the albums that Elvis had recorded and played them non-stop. As a result, even at six years old, I knew most of the lyrics by heart.

My sisters had purchased tickets for the concert and had chosen to take me with them at my request. I was very excited and did not know quite what to expect, but once we got there, the experience had such an impact on me, that now, in my forties, I can still recall most of the event with vivid detail.

We sat toward the back, but there were plenty of flashing lights throughout the arena. Every seat was sold out. Everyone was waiting with anticipation. The music began to play about fifteen minutes before the start of the show. It grew louder and louder, and our anticipation grew right along with it. The lights began to flash brighter and faster, the closer it got to when "The King" would take the stage. They brought out more and more band members, more and more back-up singers, increased the lights more and more, and let the music crash to a resounding crescendo.

At that point, Elvis Presley's famous introduction began to play. The volume went up and up and up—and increased until the crowd was almost in an ecstatic frenzy, waiting for their hero to take the stage. Elvis Presley came out onto the stage wearing his classic bell-bottoms, with sequins on his jumpsuit, a large collar, and his well-known sideburns. I recall what he looked like more from the album covers than in person because we were so far away we could hardly make out the detail.

Nonetheless, the crowd around us at the back of that arena was ecstatic. Girls and guys alike were jumping up and down, screaming: "Elvis! Elvis! Elvis! Elvis! Elvis!" That went on through the entire show, sometimes louder and sometimes softer, as Elvis sang fast songs or slow songs, loud songs or quiet songs. He moved our emotions with his voice, volume, and tempo. He had everyone eating out of the palm of his hand. When he finished a slow or quiet song, he would transition into a loud and fast-moving song. As he did so, the crowd would respond accordingly with louder and louder chants of "Elvis! Elvis! Elvis!"

At the end, in classic Elvis Presley concert style, the music continued to play until Elvis had left the stage. We were left to wonder: Would Elvis return? He made two encore appearances that night, and the crowd went absolutely wild each time. After the second encore, Elvis left the stage and we were all in wonder for several minutes. Would he come back on stage a third time?

Then came that famous phrase, "Elvis has left the building."

With that, the crowd reached crescendo again. These visions came back to me as Wayne talked about the many motivational speakers that he had hired to speak to his Fortune 500 company. I told him that I had been at an Elvis Presley concert, and I recalled to him several of the details that I just described to you.

Wayne said, "That's exactly what I'm talking about!" as he tapped the front of my shoulder in a gentle fashion. "With these motivational speakers, there was a lot of hype, a lot of energy, a lot of music, a lot of passion," he said. "But it was much like going to a concert by someone like Elvis, when he was so popular. His songs were only a few minutes long and probably didn't have much meaning beyond some cute rhyming lyrics."

"A day or two after the concert, how did you feel about your experience seeing Elvis Presley?" he asked.

"Well, I guess it was over kind of fast, when I think about it," I said. "The next day, the hype was gone and life went back to normal."

He smiled and said, "That's exactly the experience I'm talking about. We spent thousands of dollars on these speakers in the 1970s and '80s, and there was a great deal of hype and excitement, but after they left, there wasn't much there to sustain it. There was no depth of quality to the program other than its entertainment value."

"That's interesting," I said. "Why do you suppose that industry began to fade? There are still motivational speakers, but not to the same extent or in the same way as in the '70s, the '80s, or even the early '90s."

"There is an easy answer to that," he said. Again, I admired his insight and intellect as one who had stayed with his company for his entire career. He had risen from account executive to CEO and had taken early retirement with a very nice legacy left behind.

"The motivational speakers," he continued, "were so effective at this temporary hype that managers often mistook or misunderstood its lasting value. They thought they could do the same type of thing as executives. As a result, they would try to coach these types of meetings themselves and manage by the same principle of motivation."

"That doesn't seem like it would work," I said.

"You're exactly right," he continued. "The company got temporary allegiance from its employees, but the executives didn't see the employees as team members or people who could truly make a difference in the company. They were being groomed simply to do what they were told and to try to do it well. That's not effective leadership."

He then went on to explain: "The most effective leaders that I've seen and that I've experienced, Chris, were those that stopped trying to influence from *without* and started trying to influence from *within*."

"I hear the terms, but I'm not sure I quite understand the concepts," I said.

"The motivational speakers got people to laugh or almost cry, based on how they were affected from outside. They followed directions like a group of people being influenced simply by stimuli. And that is exactly what it was— temporary stimuli. Effective leaders who have really made a difference have made people think," he said.

"They have given them something of substance—a real take-home value, either from the company meeting or from a staff gathering. They've given them a vote of confidence. They've believed in them. They've inspired their creativity and made them want to find the right answers and carry out their own actions. That's the difference between motivation and inspiration."

"It sounds like one is temporary, and one is lasting," I said.

"That's exactly right," he added.

Having studied management for many years, I had seen the rise and fall of many middle and senior managers as described in books and the pages of the *Wall Street Journal*, *Forbes*, *Fortune*, and similar publications. There was a quality that made some individuals able to continue in the same workplace—instead of being replaced, they were promoted. Wayne struck me as that type of person. I felt that our relationship was close enough that I could explain that to him and ask if he felt that described him. Wayne is a humble man, but also a very accomplished executive who has risen to the ranks that only few in our country do. I knew he would give me an honest answer.

"Chris, let me explain it this way," he said. "Have you ever read the book *Iacocca*?"

"Sure," I said. "I read it the year it came out."

"Well, I have had the chance to be at meetings with Lee Iacocca," he said. "While he may not have gotten along too well with certain members of the Ford family, he was a long-term success at Chrysler. Why do you think that is?"

"Based on our conversation," I said, "I'm guessing that's because he inspired rather than motivated?"

"That's exactly right," he said, gently pointing his finger at my chest. "You've hit the nail on the head. He inspired people to want to be part of something bigger than themselves. He encouraged them to be members of a team. Although he has a powerful personality, when I heard him speak, Chris, he spoke to them as someone who was 'on their team.' He would tell them how much he valued them. He would paint a picture for them of what could be possible, and he would invite them to make their own unique contribution. To me, that's inspiration."

"It sounds to me, Wayne, as if you learned a great deal from him, or you were probably already practicing it for yourself."

"I think I was to a large extent, and that's why my company

continued to grow. But I think that being a leader means you are always growing as a leader and as a person," he said. "That was always one of the traits I admired—and still admire—about Lee Iacocca."

Due to the openness of our friendship, I responded, "That's one of the things I've always respected—and continue to respect and admire—about you, Wayne."

The conversation with him proves a point: The most effective leaders do not try to influence from the outside, but from the inside. They try to help people to create their own drive, find their own switches, and discover their own reasons for doing what they do. When they are capable of doing this, people will continue on a pathway of steady growth long after a meeting is over—and for weeks, months, and years to come, if they truly understand what drives them and where their inspiration comes from.

As I look back on the past three years of speaking engagements, training sessions, seminars, and corporate retreats I've been asked to lead, I can identify a recurring theme with each new inquiry. We get many unsolicited phone calls and referrals from individuals who have seen me speak, or seen the effect of our training programs on other companies, and would like to experience the same results. Or perhaps their friends and co-workers, associates and other peers, have directed them to us, and they ask if we can speak or train with them as well.

Inevitably, I hear a comment like this: "Chris, I know the quality of your programs from what I was told, but I want to make sure our people have a *take-home value.* We've spent far too much money on motivational speakers who offer a lot of hype but very little substance."

My response is always the same: "We've been studying this for several years, and I could not agree more. My personal promise is that everyone in your room will leave with the opportunity to implement ten or fifteen new ideas starting immediately, if they choose. But the choice is theirs."

"That's exactly what we're looking for," comes the response every time.

What does this tell us about the landscape of effective leadership in corporate America today? It tells us that corporate America and individuals at the everyday level are not looking for the next quick-fix. We've had enough of those. People who want to take ownership in their lives and become effective leaders want to be taught how to do it on their own. They want to be given tools and techniques that they can implement to create strategies that make lasting differences.

How about you? Are you an individual who wants to achieve effective leadership, and are you ready to actually implement the concepts and ideas in this book? If you are, I would suggest the following: As you seek to be a leader by design, not default, don't try to simply motivate the people around you at work, or even at home. Instead, try to get them to be inspired. Try to give them tools and ideas to help them live a better life and build a better person out of themselves to achieve a greater level of happiness.

Leave the temporary entertaining to the "Elvis Presley" types of today. That is what they do. That is what they provide. They are in the business of temporary entertainment, and some of them make tremendous livings because they are very good at it. Leave the temporary to them. *Instead of motivating others to temporary excitement, inspire them to permanent change for the better.*

How is this done? The answer is simple, and we've already discussed it in this book. Help them to concentrate not on *how* to do something but *why*. Whether one employee is filling in a shift for another, your child is cleaning his or her room, or your husband or wife is taking time to slow down and spend some time with you...truly invite them to examine not *how* to accomplish something, but *why* they should, or would, want to. As an effective leader, you'll have moved past motivation to create an atmosphere and opportunity for true inspiration.

Here is an example. Recently I was on the phone with one of the business owners for whom I am a life coach. His name is

Ken, and he is a veteran Snap-on tool representative. He is a true entrepreneur and quite good at it. Ken is also very involved with the praise band at his church. He is good at playing the music and in selecting it as well.

During our coaching session, we began to talk about the "how" and the "why" of life. I explained to him that those who know the "how" usually work for those who know the "why."

"What's the difference?" he asked.

"The 'how' is simply a way in which something is done," I explained. "It is very much like directions to get somewhere or instructions to complete a project."

"So what is the 'why?' " he asked, even though I believe he knew the answer but merely wanted it reinforced.

"The 'why,' Ken, is the reason that the directions or the instructions are followed."

"So the 'why' really keeps the bigger picture in mind?" he asked.

"Exactly," I affirmed.

"Right now, I am preparing for the Christmas season at our church by arranging the music that the band will play. It isn't too difficult; you pick the music that you know that people will like and can sing. I'm putting a lot of time into it, though, and I think it is because of the 'why.' "

"What do you mean?" I asked.

"Well, I am putting time in because ultimately I don't want people to be 'Christmassed out' by the time the actual day comes. I am trying to creatively mix it up with Christmas and non-Christmas songs."

"Why don't you try switching up a little Richard Simmons *Sweatin' to the Oldies* with Willie Nelson's *Whiskey for My Men, Beer for My Horses?"* I suggested.

After he stopped laughing, he said, "That really wasn't what I had in mind."

"Perhaps a little Slim Pickens with just a dash of The Bee Gees and just a bit of Boy George."

"That combination is wrong for many, many reasons," he said with a chuckle. "What I mean, Chris, is that the 'why' of spending so much time is that I want a good outcome. I want them to have a lasting impression of the season, not just a temporary worship service."

"That's exactly right!" I affirmed. "The more that you can keep your eye on the long-term inspirations, the 'why,' if you will, the easier the 'how' becomes. When you keep an eye on why you are doing what you are doing, you'll naturally find a way to do it better—more efficiently or more effectively."

"Okay, since we understand the topic, just out of curiosity, how would you apply this to my Snap-on business?"

"How would you?" I asked.

"Well, I would start by asking the 'why.' "

"What does that tell you?"

"Well, I'm in business for myself to have an unlimited opportunity, my own schedule, and the chance to cultivate and develop new relationships."

"Is there anything else?"

"What do you mean?" he asked.

"Why are you doing what you are doing?"

"You mean Snap-on specifically?" he asked.

"Exactly."

"I like tools, I like cars, and I like people. I believe that Snap-on has a good product that I feel good about representing," he offered.

"Why do you feel good about it? I mean, what is the 'why?' "

"What do you mean?"

"Who is the ultimate recipient?" I asked.

"The mechanic, right?"

"Do you really think so?" I asked, begging the question.

"When you phrase it that way, I'm not so sure," he added with an audible grin.

"Whose car ultimately gets worked on?" I asked.

"The client of the mechanic," he stated with confidence.

"So, when Mom is trying to take little Suzie and Johnny to school and it is cold in the Chicago area, is it important that their car not break down?" I asked, leading the application.

"Of course," he affirmed.

"Then the end-user is ultimately the mom with the safe kids because you had the tools to provide to their mechanic."

"Wow! What an insight," he said, his voice rising in volume and tone. "I've never thought of it that way before. Can you help me apply this now?" he requested.

"Well, when you think of the 'why' as you complete your normal sales calls, won't it help you to not just get them temporarily hyped about a product, but to get them inspired to want to do business with you long-term?"

"Sure," he agreed. "That's just good business."

"It's more than that," I offered. "It's good service. The tools may be good, but your relationships with the mechanics in the shops inspire them to want to do business with you and to do the best they can on the cars rather than rush through."

Ken got it. A light bulb went on.

He sent me an e-mail that night indicating that he had several "Aha's!" during our conversation dealing with the 'how' and the 'why' as we looked at temporary motivation vs. long-term inspiration. That is really the point of this chapter.

Communicating with the thought of inspiration vs. motivation doesn't have to be rocket surgery. If we keep in mind the end result, the long-term vision of what we want to accomplish, we will focus on the 'why.' When we do, the 'how' wonderfully becomes self-evident to us. So focus on the 'why' and the long-term, and leave the short-term motivation to those with bell-bottoms, sideburns, and jumpsuits.

Elvis has left the building! Thank you…thank you very much!

Chapter 12

Made From Clay Or A Monkey's Nephew

Focus On Your Purpose, Not On Distractions

Purpose is a powerful concept. Purpose gives us direction. Purpose, quite frankly, gives us the power to do whatever we believe that we are supposed to do. If we believe that we have a purpose, we will find a way, plan a strategy, and execute our action with intent. Knowing our purpose gives us the leverage we need to accomplish what we desire.

I don't take time to watch much television. In fact, most days I usually don't watch any, other than at the health club when I am working out on the stair stepper or treadmill. But in the limited television that I watch, I've seen commercials for the past several years that have struck me as funny and reminded me of the importance of professional purpose. Perhaps you've seen them.

The commercials are for sandwich shops franchised by a company that is popular throughout the country. They describe the head chef as someone "obsessed with his purpose," which is making great sub sandwiches. He has undying love for what he does and puts his heart and soul into it. In a funny and memorable way, these commercials demonstrate his sense of purpose.

In one commercial, the chef builds the perfect sandwich but then realizes that, although he is wearing a chef's hat, he was so obsessed with getting to work to make the sandwiches that he forgot to put on his pants. As he walks away, we see that he is sporting polka-dotted boxer shorts with black socks and shoes. It is a cute, memorable way to express the point.

In another commercial, as he leaves for work, you see that

parts of his lawn have been scorched by the sun while other parts are greatly overgrown. His house looks like no one has lived there for years because he has spent all his time thinking about creating the perfect sandwiches for this sandwich chain.

Another example from television involves one of my favorite characters from *The Andy Griffith Show*, Barney Fife, and how clearly he knows his purpose. Barney Fife knows that he is to "serve and protect." He takes it very seriously, sometimes, in a very comedic way, almost too seriously.

In one episode, Barney disguises himself as a bush with tied-on branches, twigs, and leaves. His goal is to catch truck drivers who are speeding five miles over the speed limit to make it up the next hill. Over time, Sheriff Andy Taylor convinces him that the truckers need that speed or they won't be able to make it up the hill, and Barney agrees. His character is fun (and funny), and the writers did a great job of describing someone who totally gets his purpose. Now, we may not disguise ourselves as a bush and tie on branches, but understanding our purpose makes a great difference in our lives.

I have seen a huge difference in purpose between individuals who believe they simply have a job vs. those who have a career. A job is a place that you go to provide meals for a family and clothing for our bodies. A career is a job taken to the next level. In a career we have worked and honed our skills to be valuable to the company or industry to make sure that we have job security. Perhaps we even attain a certain level of respect from other people.

We spend more time at work than at home, so work should not be a place that we hate. There shouldn't be much of a difference between Saturday and Monday. In the case of Barney Fife, he rarely seemed to be off duty. Right or wrong, why was that? The reason was because he knew his purpose and took it with him wherever he went.

However you feel that you came to be, evolution or creation, it doesn't really matter for purposes of this chapter. You are here. You have a purpose. You physically, emotionally, spiritually, and intellectually exist on planet Earth. This is true, unless you work for NASA and are reading this aboard the International Space Station. In that case all bets, and gravity, are off. As someone living on Earth, however, let me ask you a simple yet profound question: What is your purpose? Another way to say it is: Why are you here?

As we prepared to collect research and write this easy-to-read guide, we realized that we needed to include one very important topic; the concept of "purpose." If you don't know your purpose, it doesn't matter what ideas you take from this book. None of them will stick. If you understand and embrace your personal sense of purpose, the ideas in this book will completely empower you. The strategies and concepts will supercharge your life as you reach for the stars.

Purpose can be defined as the reason for which something exists or is accomplished, the logical expected outcome, or the end result. Understanding this definition, we can ask ourselves, "What is my purpose?" or "Why am I here?" Once each of us discovers the answer to this key question, everything else falls into place.

We would like to invite you to examine and understand your purpose in three areas because essentially you have three purposes:

1. A General Purpose.
2. A Personal Purpose.
3. A Professional Purpose.

Understanding your General Purpose

Let me ask you the same question again: Why are you here? Why are you on planet Earth? This is not a religious question. It really doesn't matter whether you believe that we evolved from apes or were created by an all-powerful God, or both. I have my views on how we came to be here, and I have my beliefs. I firmly hold them, but that's not the issue. In this chapter, it's not *how* we got here, but *why* we are here that we'd like you to consider.

Understanding your *general purpose* may mean you believe that you are here to give as much back to society as you can. Or you may believe that you are here to get as much from society as you can in the short time that you are alive. With either of those very different views of why you believe you're here, your purpose will dictate how you act and interact.

So why are you here? What is your purpose? You were created special and wonderful. You have a unique set of abilities. You may share several things in common with someone else. You may even have a twin brother or sister whom you look very much like. Even so, there are differences between you.

You were created to be uniquely you. Isn't that wonderful? Your purpose—why you feel you are here—will greatly determine and shape how you spend your time on this planet. It will determine what you focus on and where you expend your energy. So, what is that purpose?

To help answer that question, if you have not already done so, envision this: What would life be like for the people around you if you were not here? What if you never existed? What if you were never born? What if you, with your specific set of genetic abilities, psychological makeup, and personality traits, never came to be on planet Earth? How would the Earth be different?

You might answer this in different ways depending on the level of self-confidence that you have. But if you're really honest with yourself, regardless of your self-confidence, you can picture the lives of the people closest to you being different in some way. Perhaps if you have more self-confidence, you might think about the lives of many other people that you affect by being alive. You have significance for them, and life would be very different for them in some way if you were not alive or had not been born.

We may not all have the same opportunity as James Stewart's

character George Bailey in the movie *It's a Wonderful Life.* We are unlikely to have an angel show us what the world would be like if we had not been born. Nonetheless, we can examine the relationships we have with others. We can examine what we have contributed to their lives—or perhaps are contributing now.

The people, today and throughout history, who have most clearly understood their general purpose have understood that they were born with an ability to contribute. Those who most fully understand this go a step further and develop a desire to serve. They see themselves as part of a continuum rather than as an isolated island. They understand that they are here to make a difference. In doing so, they grasp an understanding of their purpose.

You don't have to overcomplicate your general purpose. It can be quite simple. You might say something as simple as you are here to make the world a better place. It could be to let your family know that they are loved. Great! If that's the case, we can examine in your personal and professional purpose how you can do that.

Once you know your purpose, you can prioritize the tasks that come your way. That doesn't have to be *Rocket Surgery.* When tasks or assignments come your way, ask yourself if they fit into your general purpose. If they do, great. Do them with all of your might. If they don't, examine how often these types of tasks come your way. If they come your way regularly, you may need to ask yourself if you are personally or professionally where you need to be. This leads to our second examination of purpose.

Understanding Your Personal Purpose

To understand your *personal purpose,* ask yourself what you add or contribute to the lives of those who are closest to you. That can be your mother or father, husband or wife, sister or brother, son, daughter, friend, parole officer (just checking to see if you are awake here), or anyone else who's close to you. What is your personal purpose? In other words, what does it mean when you get up in the morning, alive for another day and present in their lives? What do you have to contribute and give back to them that is unique to you?

Personal purpose makes many other things in our lives take a backseat—or second place, so to speak. I have often said in my personal excellence seminars that my primary personal purpose in life is to make sure that my wife Julie feels happy, loved, cared for, and provided for, and also to make sure that our children, Connor and Kelsey, have a loving, safe environment where they can grow and be nurtured. That's my personal purpose.

What's your personal purpose? How you define your personal purpose will shape and determine the actions that you take, the priorities that you establish, and the schedule that you keep. For example, my personal purpose means providing for Julie and our children—not just financially, but also in terms of love, security, protection, great reputation, and fun lifestyle. It means that I work to keep our company going, to keep bills paid, to save for retirement, and to save for college.

Beyond that, it means that I make sure to exercise five times per week. That way my body stays healthy. I can live a long time and experience many more years to come with Julie and watch our children grow. It also means, in the short-term, that I am going to work efficiently. I will establish my priorities and master my schedule. I will use my time in such a way that I am on time for dinner most nights—ensuring that I have worked hard and smart enough during the week that I can take time on the weekend to go hiking with my family or play basketball and baseball.

When you understand your personal purpose, the priorities and tasks of your life begin to take their shape and place rather quickly. Picture it like building something with papier-maché. When we were in grade school, we had the opportunity to work with papier-maché. What did we do? We started with the raw material—like wire—and shaped it into a cone or a stand or an elephant or a rocket or something else; you could not quite tell what it was at first. We just had an idea. Next, we took paper and the wet, gooey papier-maché, mixed them together, and then put them on one sheet at a time. As each layer began to dry, the next one was added until at last we had a project that we had created step-by-step.

Understanding our purposes in life is very much the same way. Our general purpose forms the base structure. Our personal purpose is the next layer of the model. Our professional purpose is the last layer. They literally build on each other. We have invited you to examine why you are on this Earth and then to identify the people who are close to you in your personal life. What gives you purpose? As you can see, we are beginning to create our own model for personal excellence. You are building a better future for yourself, similar to building that papier-maché model.

I know you're going to find the process increasingly fun. I know because I have personally experienced it. Julie and I could not have started our company or successfully given seminars if we did not understand these insights ourselves. Giving advice is easy; living it is the hard part. I'm not saying we are perfect or have attained personal excellence at the highest level. As I have said, it is a journey. We are perhaps further along on that journey than some others. That is not because we are better or worse than anyone else. It simply means we have had more time to work on ourselves and to build a personal excellence model for our lives.

Wherever you are starting today, that is okay. You have taken an important step toward building personal excellence in your life. Congratulations! A journey of a thousand steps begins with a single step. The last thing this book should be is one more thing on your to-do list. We are not asking you to take on yet another task. Rather, we are inviting you to examine your sense of purpose as a concept that frees you, instead of encumbering you. It is not a task that you have to dread. You don't need to say, "Wednesdays are looking good; I will note in my day-planner that I'm going to find my purpose in life over lunch." I wish we could show you before-and-after shots of your life and the difference it makes when you truly understand and own your sense of purpose.

Knowing your personal purpose can give you lasting joy. It allows you to surround yourself with who and what is important to you. It gives you ultimate personal freedom.

Understanding Your Professional Purpose

Professional purpose goes beyond having a job and a career. A professional purpose causes us to ask ourselves, "Am I engaged in employment that will help me give back to the world in the best possible way?" Understanding of our professional purpose means the difference between having temporary happiness and lasting joy.

A much-quoted example that has been used in many books, articles, and programs is that of Thomas Edison. He made one thousand attempts at creating the first light bulb before one actually worked. His purpose was to create a bulb that would light and stay lit, thus providing light to a room. When Edison finished making the one that finally worked, a reporter asked him, "Mr. Edison, how does it feel to have failed one thousand times before becoming successful?"

He replied, "My good man, I did not fail one thousand times. I was successful in finding one thousand ways the light bulb would not work."

What if Thomas Edison had had no professional purpose? What if he had confused happiness and joy and merely went to work for the sake of going to work? Surely he or anyone else who felt that way would have given up long, long before one thousand attempts. His professional purpose was to make that light bulb work.

Maybe your professional purpose is to create something—a product, an invention, or a company. Maybe it is simply to do the best you can where you are. But I can tell you this: Your attitude will be a result of how you feel in your profession, whether you truly have purpose or not. Two examples come to my mind. Neither is glamorous, but both prove a point.

We lived in an affluent suburb just north of Milwaukee and close to Lake Michigan. As such, we often got what is called "lake-effect snow." The lake draws in the clouds, producing much heavier snow than in other areas. One winter, we got a particularly heavy snow. The snow fell in a short time, piling up everywhere and causing many people to have to shovel or snow-blow, or simply wait until someone else would come and dig them out.

A big, orange truck turned the corner to come down the cul-de-sac where we lived. It was a dump truck with a plow on the front and salt in the back, very typical of Midwestern snow clearing. The gentleman driving the truck, who I recognized but did not know very well, gave a wave and smiled. As I was cleaning our walk, I yelled in a friendly voice, "Someone's having a great day!"

"I'm moving some snow," he said, "and I love it!"

As he turned the corner of our cul-de-sac and slowed his truck, I flagged him down. "Good morning!" I said.

"It certainly is," he said with a smile on his face.

I said, "I've seen you before, and I'm very grateful for what you are doing. But I have a question for you."

"Shoot," he said with another smile.

"I do personal excellence training and strategy coaching for a living. I can't help but notice that while other people seem to be frustrated, you're in a great mood. Why is that?"

"Because I like what I do," he said.

"I was hoping that would be the answer," I said. "Otherwise, we might have to call the Human Resource Department and take some blood tests."

He laughed.

"But seriously, what is it about your career that you enjoy?" I did not use the word "job" because I didn't want to trivialize what he did and enjoyed so much, as can often happen with that word.

"I get to help keep people safe," he said with a smile. "I am helping kids get to school, school buses get to the kids, and mommies and daddies get to work."

"You must be a father," I said.

"Sure am," he said. "I have three of my own."

Not wanting to hold him up as the snow was still falling heavily, I said, "You're doing a great job. Keep it up, partner."

"Thanks," he said. "Have a great day!"

As I continued to clear our walkway, I thought about that. I thought about the fact that he enjoyed what he did because it gave him the professional purpose of helping others and the personal purpose of providing for his family. Just from that brief conversation, I understood that he got it. He understood! At some level, purpose meant something to him. I smiled and continued to clear the walk, thinking about my own life and my own purposes.

The second example occurred just yesterday. I went to the local hardware store to buy three bolts for our motor scooter. The scooter works fine and is a great toy for our family, but if the kickstand doesn't work, you can't stand it up when you're not riding it. Therefore, three inexpensive and seemingly insignificant bolts were very important.

When I walked into the hardware store, I was greeted by a friendly woman wearing a blue vest that displayed the name of the store.

"How may I help you? Looks like you need something," she said with a smile.

"I need three bolts, please."

She looked at the one I'd brought and immediately told me the size she thought they were. She held it up to the light and squinted, looked at me, smiled, and said, "Not sure, but it could be metric. Let's find out together."

As we walked back to the aisle, I was taken by how involved

and friendly she was. In the short time that we were standing there, I explained to her what the bolts were for, and she indicated that several other individuals had been in looking for that same bolt for their motor scooters.

"Must be some kind of manufacturing defect," she said with a smile. "Here you go; here are your bolts." She handed them to me.

As we walked back to the front, we talked very briefly, but in that short time, I found out that she had been working at that hardware store for ten years, been married for twenty-six years, had children, and absolutely loved what she did.

"May I ask you a question?" I inquired.

"Absolutely," she said. "Anything you want."

The comedic side of me wanted to ask her a differential calculus question. But keeping on track, I said, "You seem to really enjoy what you do. May I ask why? Before you answer, let me say that I really enjoy hearing from people who find joy in what they do."

She put it simply and to the point: "I help people find solutions for challenges that they face. I find joy in sending them home knowing I've done the best job I could do."

Isn't that wonderful! Isn't that simple! Ideally, I hope that each person, including us as authors, has that same simplistic and professional purpose in life. To enjoy helping people find solutions to challenges they face—what a great statement of professional purpose! If we all do this in the world in general, with those who are closest to us, and with those whom we have the privilege to serve through our employment, we can truly begin to understand the power of purpose.

Understanding Their Purpose Makes Leaders Effective

When we fully understand our purpose, we begin to make decisions about how we are going to live out that purpose. These decisions lead to action, which ultimately produces the results that we desire and deserve. Nothing is accomplished without action, and of course, we only take action after we or someone else decide to put something into motion. When we understand desired outcomes—the "why"—before taking actions, the actions themselves become much easier.

I am regularly invited into various organizations to assist them with my expertise and strategic planning. What we do most effectively for companies is to train and educate individuals in personal excellence. We identify areas that need correction and then use our techniques and strategies to help individuals achieve new levels of personal excellence and effective leadership...if they choose.

The last part of that sentence is the most key: "if they choose." You cannot make anyone choose to be a leader. You cannot make anyone choose to seek out and take ownership of their purpose. You can show them the way, but ultimately the decision must be theirs. When we work with a company and its employees, we are immediately able to determine if its leaders understand their purpose, or at least their professional purpose, by how they address outcomes. By evaluating how they describe their current situation or, more importantly, how they arrived at their current situation, we are able to make this distinction.

This holds true not only in the workplace, but also in life. By using the concepts in this chapter, you also should be able to determine immediately whether an individual is an effective leader, too. It becomes very simple. Effective leaders who understand their professional purpose also follow these rules of leadership:

Rule 1: When plans fail, the effective leader takes responsibility.

Rule 2: When success is achieved or outcomes are beneficial to everyone's progress, the effective leader shares the credit with others.

Rule 3: When success is desired, effective leaders empower others to soar.

Rule 4: When success is achieved, effective leaders celebrate with those who make it possible.

Rule 5: When success is achieved, effective leaders study why so that it can be replicated.

These simple moments of truth show whether the leader truly understands his or her professional purpose as a leader. Leaders must build teams over time through relationships. And that brings up another point—the importance of understanding time as it relates to effective leadership. Individuals often grow and mature slowly at this point in their journey of personal excellence and rise in a gradually ascending fashion to a place of effective leadership.

Like personal excellence, effective leadership is a journey, not a destination. The more leaders learn, experience, and open their minds, the more they continue to grow and become more effective. But not all progress toward effective leadership takes place slowly. In some instances, the individual has repeated the same pattern, experienced the same result, and then had what we call an "Aha!" moment.

These moments often come as a result of something major that happened. Sometimes, "Aha!" moments come when the leader reviews a recent success and examines what thoughts, steps, and actions made that outcome a reality. More often than not, however, "Aha!" moments take place at times of failure or perceived failure. Failing to reach a desired outcome—or reaching an unexpected or negative outcome—can produce some of the quickest and most dramatic changes in a leader's ability to increase his or her effectiveness. Whether the "Aha!" is because the leader has realized something he or she would like to repeat or a mistake he or she now knows how to avoid, the greatest insights come when the leader understands how that outcome relates to his or her own professional purpose. In other words, it happens when he or she connects the outcome to the bigger picture. As we write the final draft of this book and prepare for editing and publishing, an example of this came to mind.

The other night, Julie and I had a few extra moments at the end of the day and spent them watching the Country Music Association Awards on television. As a person who teaches personal excellence and high-performance leadership, I thoroughly enjoy hearing acceptance speeches, no matter how brief. The speeches that tell me the most about the person or group as a leader or leaders are the ones that quickly list the many people who have helped the winner achieve success.

When we turned on the show, the group Rascal Flatts was receiving an award. The reason they got the award wasn't important to me; I just wanted to hear their acceptance speech. The members of the group took the stage and began to quickly thank a list that included writers, producers, directors, record labels, spouses, and friends.

As I listened to the speech, I noticed that at no time had they said how great they sang, how hard they worked, or the sacrifices they made. Instead, they talked about the people who were so instrumental in helping them to accomplish what they feel is their professional purpose. They didn't use the words "professional purpose," but the concept was certainly the same.

At one point, a member of the band perfectly summed up what I consider to be effective leadership in that type of situation. He held up the award and, after his band members had listed the many people responsible, he said, "We want to thank each and every one of you. This award is really yours as much as it is ours. Thank you, and God bless."

That is the type of attitude we are talking about in effective leadership. Individuals in the spotlight—in this case, a music group—stood up and became effective leaders. The artists expressed gratitude and appreciation for all the people who had made their award possible. They expressed the fact that they would not be standing there without a team effort.

As we begin to more fully understand effective leadership, each of us would do well to look at current outcomes and categorize them as negative or positive. If they are negative and we contributed to that, being an effective leader means taking responsibility and offering a sincere effort to redirect future outcomes or make the situation right, if possible. In the situations where we experience terrific outcomes or great accomplishments, being an effective leader means thinking immediately of those individuals who helped this take place and showing them our sincere gratitude and appreciation in a personal sense—and whenever possible in a public setting.

In this chapter we learned a valuable lesson. Leaders are not made effective by the title on the doorway to their office. Leaders are made effective by the responsibility they take and the credit they share. They become effective by taking a big-picture view and knowing their sense of purpose. A star leader asks himself or herself many questions. How can I be a better leader? What is my purpose? Am I making decisions and communicating to others with my purpose in mind? Is my understanding of my purpose empowering me to build a sense of team with others?

As we summarize this chapter on purpose, let's make it very simple. Think of your life as having two sections: home life and professional life. Each has its purpose, personal or professional, and everyone can improve somewhere. Life is a journey. As a child, I used to think that I would have nothing left to learn as an adult, because I would already know everything. Now that I am an adult, I have learned that I never want to stop learning. I learn from watching others. I learn from reading book-after-book. I learn from my successes. I learn from my failures.

My pattern is to always look for things to tweak. Perhaps it is something as simple as learning to put the coffee in the coffeepot the night before. I have learned that a few minutes at night equal twice the time in the morning. That might sound silly, but that one little act helps me to be a better leader in my home. It enables me to be happier in the morning because I love my coffee, and it's ready for me when I want it. This, in turn, allows me to be happier with my family. That allows me to empower them to start their day on a happy note and to fulfill my personal purpose as a husband and a father.

My coffeepot example may sound silly to you, but not to me. (Okay, so I may have caffeine issues and, yes, I have always had that nervous twitch.) On a serious note, and in conclusion, let me say that our understanding of purpose in our lives will guide the decisions and actions that we take. As we discussed in the last chapter, when we truly understand the "why" in our lives, the "how" seems to fall into place. And when we truly understand our purpose, we will find a way to accomplish our tasks and reach our objectives. This is what star leaders do very effectively, and it is something that you can start today!

CHAPTER 13

SCREAMING...YET QUIETLY

CREATING COMMUNICATION WITH PURPOSE

Many of us can probably remember television commercials from the mid-'80s for package delivery companies, telephone companies, and other entities that showed the prematurely balding boss sitting behind a desk twice the size of reality in his three-piece suit with a large gold ring and a cigar sticking out of his mouth as he screamed, "Johnson, get in here! I need to see you!"

In those commercials, indicative of the style of leadership at the time, the boss was over-bearing and demanding. He spoke in short directives, often raising his voice and demanding results with little input required or requested from the employee, who usually was standing across from the desk with stooped shoulders, short-sleeved shirt and tie, and hair tossed in a sweaty, nervous fashion, hoping he wouldn't get reprimanded again or fired. They were silly and fun commercials and obviously good marketing because many of us can still recall them twenty-plus years later.

The sad reality is that the commercials were effective because they got at the heart of how the "average person" felt—beaten down often by upper management or other people in leadership positions in their life. The marketing spin, or desired effectiveness, for the commercials was to have the viewer feel a common bond with the downtrodden employee. The advertising company would then provide the solution to help them overcome the overbearing situation or person and achieve the joy or happiness that they deserved.

Studies have indicated that these commercials were highly

effective in creating or eliciting a response from the consumer. This display of the average person's experience with his or her leader's communications caused product sales and services to continue to go up.

Times have changed greatly since then. Those types of leaders often did not last very long. There are exceptions to every rule, but generally those individuals did not gain a steady following and create a team of long-term employees whose loyalties were commendable.

Instead, the culture and climate in corporate America began to turn. Things began to change in the landscape of longevity in the workplace. People began to jump ship. They went looking for another atmosphere or opportunity where the leader would have better communication skills and value them more as a person. This is not surprising. Communication is key to leading effectively.

I can still recall undertaking my doctoral studies in psychotherapy and human interaction in the early '90s. As part of the clinical work, we had to observe and take notes while other psychotherapists and mental health professionals listened to, and addressed, the challenges and problems of their patients.

An observation that quickly became clear was that a lack of communication was at the heart of many of the relationship breakdowns. We weren't dealing with corporate America. These were husbands and wives. These were family members and in-laws. These were friends, neighbors, and other individuals outside the workplace. And at the heart of many of their challenges in relationships and bridge building was a lack of effective communication.

This intrigued me. I had now seen and observed it from both sides. I had seen it in corporate America, as indicated by the marketing spin of the commercials, and I had seen it on the personal level through the clinical work of my doctorate studies. I was not only intrigued, I was fascinated.

I began to ask myself: Could relationship opportunities and

effective leadership really be as simple as communication? I soon discovered that the answer is a resounding yes.

After my automobile accident, Julie and I began to study effective leaders in our society. We found that communication truly is at the heart of effective leadership. We observed the interactions among the doctors and the nurses at the hospital in Brookfield, Wisconsin, where I was recovering. We began to notice that many of the doctors had very similar credentials. They might practice different specialties, work for different medical practices, and have different opportunities to contribute from their unique talents, but, by and large, they had roughly the same amount of education. They were basically on the same level field. We noticed the same situation with the nurses. Some worked in maternity, while others were in spinal injuries, such as the area where I was. Still others were in the emergency room. But, by and large, they all had similar credentials. Those were the similarities, but what we noticed most were the differences.

We noticed that, despite their similar credentials, the doctors had greatly varying levels of effectiveness. The ones who had the best effect on the patients and the most productive interactions with other doctors and nurses were those who had the best communication skills. The nurses who seemed to have an internal joy—despite stressed-out situations, a heavy workload, or an unforeseen circumstance—were those who had great communication skills. We noticed the same thing on basically every level of the hospital staff. The individuals that seemed to have the most joy, be the most effective leaders, and make the biggest difference with their peers and patients were those with the greatest communication skills.

That was a key component of why I am walking today. I give glory to God for the gift of being able to walk again, and I have to say that it took a tremendous amount of self-determination. Certainly I could not have done it without Julie's support and love. But, one other individual made a difference. That was my attending physician. He introduced us to neurosciences, neuro-programming, and the mind-body connection.

He was a very busy surgeon, an expert in spinal injuries and highly in-demand. He was consistently being asked to go from place to place, take long-distance phone calls with questions, and answer inquiries from nurses and other doctors. Yet, despite all these requests, he took time to sit with me whenever he visited the room or at least stand by the bed for longer than I expected.

He would ask me questions about how I felt and listen intently to my responses. He would then smile and share with me that individuals with my type of injury usually do not walk again. However, many times they can, he said, and the difference is how they communicate with themselves. He taught me a life-changing lesson. *Communication with yourself is key.* You are the leader of your own life. The better you can communicate with yourself, the better you will be able to communicate with others.

As we continued to study individuals who were effective leaders because they were effective communicators, we found three key components to effective communication. These three were present in everyone we studied, and we have continued to find them universally true. *Effective leaders who communicate the best do four things*:

1. They communicate with purpose.
2. They communicate with meaning.
3. They communicate with intention.
4. They communicate with conviction and authority.

Let's examine the importance of each of these so that we can all rise to a new level of excellence in our communications, effectiveness, and leadership.

Communicate with Purpose

As we discussed earlier, purpose can be defined as a reason, substantiation or, quite simply, why something is done. *Effective leaders communicate for a reason.* And let's not limit communication to just the verbal kind. Communication includes eye contact, listening, and repeating back to show you understand what the other person is saying and perhaps even feel it. *Effective leaders that communicate with purpose have a reason for most, if not all, of the things that they say and ideas they express.* This does not happen naturally overnight. As we stated earlier, becoming an effective leader is a journey. No one wakes up one day, stands on the bed in their bunny slippers and robe, points their finger at the ceiling smiling, with sleep lines and pillow hair, and says, "Wow! I'm an effective leader now!" Rather, effective leaders have spent time working on the necessary skills, mindset, and actions that will increase their effectiveness as leaders. Being able to communicate with purpose on a regular and consistent basis takes practice.

But doing this is quite simple. You can start today. As you interact with someone, practice this exercise: pause for just a second or two, and ask yourself why you are communicating with this person. Then ask yourself what you mean to communicate. If you do this, you will begin to practice communicating with purpose, and your communication will take on a new level of clarity, depth, and meaning. It will also produce greater and longer-lasting effects as you build relationships that will make you an effective leader.

Communicate with Meaning

Meaning can be described as a substance or a value. *Effective leaders carefully choose their words and their body-language responses to other individuals.* They communicate in a way that shows that they mean what they say. They communicate in a way that makes the other person feel special. They communicate in a way that makes the other person value what they have to say because of the thought put into it. There is a meaning behind their communication. That meaning could be a desire or intent to help. It could be to share information or to simply entertain or brighten that person's day—to bring them happiness along with their lasting joy.

Starting today, you can do a simple exercise to increase your effectiveness as a leader who communicates well. Before you speak, ask yourself not only the reason, as we discussed with purpose, but also how you intend for that person to feel after you've interacted with them. Do you intend for them to feel better than before? Ideally, every effective leader wants that outcome. *They want individuals to feel better as a result of interacting with them.*

This desired outcome will have you asking yourself what vocal tone and what type of words you plan to use. Will you, for example, use a soft tone of voice or an excited tone? Will you use words that are direct and crisp, or words that are softer? You can begin to communicate how you would like that person to feel by the type of meaning you convey. The term for this is "mirroring," something that human beings do by nature.

Those of us who have studied mirroring for years can do it more effectively, but everyone can start doing it today. As you practice, you will be able to direct and determine the outcome of the conversation and (in the best possible sense) how that person will feel as a result of interacting with you.

Communicating with Intention

Intention means an idea, feeling, or concept *leading to an outcome.* What is it that you intend this person, or yourself, to receive as a result of this interaction? Is it a compromise? Is it a solution? Is it simply an opportunity to have connected with another human being? Whatever the outcome is, that's the intention behind the communication.

Intention is different from meaning, and the two terms should not be confused. Meaning is the way you convey your words. Intention is what you expect as a result. Perhaps the intention is nothing more than building bridges, as effective leaders do on a regular basis.

A simple exercise that you can begin using today to increase the intent of your communications is asking for feedback or action. If you are asking for action, you could ask for agreement to do something. For example, when I ask my son or my daughter to clean their room, I express it this way: "Could you please clean your room so it looks nice for Mom, and I'll play with you outside in the yard when you are done. Does that sound like a great idea?" "Sure!" they say. Therefore, I have asked for an action to take place.

Perhaps you're not looking for an action but an agreement. Perhaps you're willing to say, while you are communicating with someone, that you will talk to them next week: "I will call you next Thursday. Is that all right with you?" You intend to speak with them then, and you are asking permission to agree on that. That is communicating with intention.

There is a reason why the harsh-speaking, over-bearing, and demanding managers of the commercials did not last long or have a lasting following as leaders. This type of communication is rarely, if ever, effective. Regardless of their position, the greatest leaders are those who communicate the best. As we have stated, their communication involves three things: A purpose—why were they communicating? A meaning—how did they want that person to feel as a result? And intent—what was the logical, positive outcome of this meeting, and how can they convey that?

If you take time to practice purpose once today, meaning once tomorrow, and intention once the next day, you will have completed a wonderful exercise towards dramatically increasing your ability to communicate. In doing so, you will continue further on your journey of personal excellence and dramatically increase your effectiveness as a leader.

Communicate with Conviction and Authority

Conviction and authority are distinctive qualities that also are present consistently in the communication of star leaders. Conviction and authority have very different meanings, yet when used together, they can catapult the leader's communication to an entirely different level. Let's examine what each of these terms means and why they are important.

Effective leaders communicate with *conviction.* Conviction is perhaps one of the most powerful influences. It is rooted in one's belief that something has an intrinsic value or definite outcome. A belief is something that we hold to be true no matter what. It is something that, in the deepest parts of our heart and the most basic parts of our mind, we hold to be true.

Believing something to be true is the strongest form of internal inspiration. Beliefs will cause individuals to do things far beyond their normal limitations. They will cause individuals to push themselves harder than anyone else could. Beliefs will cause individuals to search with unbounded determination until the answer or resolution is found. They will put in countless hours and unlimited energy to bring about what they believe is true or should take place.

Convictions are rooted in beliefs. While beliefs are what we hold to be true, convictions are actions that can or should take place. Conviction brings the belief to such a high level that the individual decides to take action.

For example, let me tell you about two convictions that Julie and I have regarding our children. Of course, we have many more, but these two serve as complementary examples of each other. The first conviction is that our children should complete their schoolwork, either at school or as assigned homework. They are reaching an age where homework is sent home regularly to instill routine study habits outside the classroom. They also receive homework so they can learn to work in teams with their parents and siblings and to search for answers themselves.

Our second conviction is that our children should be able to participate in sports or other extracurricular activities. We believe this makes them well-rounded and gives them the opportunity to have choices in activities besides just assigned schoolwork.

These are the beliefs on which we have decided to take action, and we have set the standards and rules. After school, homework should be done before playing. This teaches priorities and discipline. It also helps them to manage themselves and their activities since, as we will learn later in this book, no one can truly manage their time.

This conviction of availability and opportunity to do extracurricular activities means that we will let them choose activities like Little League, soccer, and swimming. Because we have such a strong conviction that they should be able to do this, we arrange our activities and manage ourselves well enough to have time to attend these events with them. Our convictions moved us to action.

Typically, due to the way our business is designed, Julie helps with most of the homework in the afternoon, and I help with some in the evening. One or both of us attend the sporting events or, if they occur at the same time, we divide and conquer. One parent goes with one child; one parent goes with the other. This is an example of beliefs causing a conviction to take action.

Effective leaders also communicate with *authority*. Authority, by definition, is position or power worthy to be able to hold an opinion. It can also be expressed as an earned right to hold a position. *Authority often has little to do with age, status, title, or other factors that normally segregate or separate individuals.* Authority can be as little or as simple as what or whom you represent.

Julie and I have such a firm conviction about our children being able to study and have extracurricular activities that we don't ask permission of our prospects or clients to maintain our schedule. We simply speak with conviction, saying that we have the opportunity to be there for our children, and authority, noting that we offer expertise in our business, so it would be within their interest as clients to work within our schedule and theirs.

In other words, we will be there for our children, and we would like to work with our clients. Therefore, with conviction and authority, we tell them, "We need to start the meeting at 3 p.m., because we must be at the soccer field by 4:30." There isn't a lot of negotiation there—and there doesn't need to be. When said in the proper, respectful tone, conviction and authority can prove immensely beneficial.

Sometimes, conviction and authority require having a tremendous amount of patience when standing your ground. One meaningful example comes to mind. Some years back, while living in the Chicago area, I observed an individual being pulled over by a police officer. An accident several miles up the road had blocked all lanes of traffic, leaving us stuck on the I-290 Eisenhower Expressway leading toward downtown Chicago.

Because it was rush hour, traffic was at its peak. Even without an accident, rush-hour congestion can make a twenty-five mile commute take two and a half hours. After several minutes of sitting in the same spot, many of us, myself included, put our cars in park and prepared for the long wait. The radio indicated where the accident was and which exits were closed; we knew we were going to be there for a while.

As I sat in traffic, lights visible out of the corner of my eye, in my rearview mirror, got my attention. I noticed the flashing, alternating blue and red lights of a police car. I also saw the alternating, flashing high beams on the front end of the car signaling its presence and arrival. Ahead of that car was a silver sport utility vehicle (SUV), driving close to the speed limit down the emergency lane. This individual had apparently lost patience with waiting along with the rest of us and decided that breaking the law and using the emergency lane for ordinary use was worth the risk. In this case, he was wrong. I sat and absorbed this entire scenario as it played out.

The officer was behind him, but the SUV driver clearly did not intend to stop. He didn't seem to be a hardened criminal trying to make a fast getaway, but rather a regular guy who was trying to exit the expressway and pretend he did not see the officer. Being a patient, laid-back person who always likes to absorb before I act, I simply watched in silence and awe.

As they approached twenty or so cars behind me and continued to drive down the emergency lane, I noticed the individuals in the cars ahead of me beginning to lose patience with the illegal driver. As I have seen happen before in Chicago, three of the drivers in the cars ahead of me nudged their cars forward until they were successfully blocking the emergency lane on the right, forcing the SUV to stop.

The timing could not have been more perfect. He was stopped exactly two car lengths behind me, so I could watch the entire story play out. I sat back, knowing I would be there for a while, and wished that I had a bowl of popcorn and a cup of soda. This was going to be an interesting show.

The man driving the SUV was upset. He began to open his door and get out of his car. Immediately, the officer's voice came over the PA system attached to the patrol car: "Sir, get back in the car."

The gentleman started to say something, but the officer cut him off and interrupted: "Sir, get back in your car and wait until I come up there."

The officer spoke with such conviction and authority that the upset gentleman immediately got back in his car. The officer exited his car and clearly was very unhappy with the situation. The man he had pulled over was in his mid-50s with a thick black mustache, receding hairline, olive-colored skin, and short but thick dark-black hair.

In contrast, the officer looked young enough that if asked when he graduated from the police academy, he could have checked his watch instead of referencing a calendar. What's more, he had a baby face and looked even younger. He looked young enough that he could have been on his way to the store to buy his first razor instead of pulling over an illegal driver.

He was built like Barney Fife and looked something like Andy Griffith's ten-year-old son Opie. He had bright, naturally orange, Irish hair and paper-white skin with countless freckles. However, make no bones about it, this officer meant business. He knew that he was an authority figure of the law, and he had the conviction that this gentleman was not going to proceed forward.

When he walked up to the car, he displayed good leadership. The gentleman in the car did not wait to be addressed. He simply started yelling at the officer in broken English, telling him where he needed to be and how he did not have time to wait. In a rare display of patience, the officer let the man groan on for what seemed like an hour, but was actually more along the lines of a minute.

When there was a break in the yelling, the officer looked at the man and sternly but calmly said, "Are you finished now, sir?" He had a very calm but very authoritative voice. It was so calm in comparison to the driver's rage that I had to laugh at the dichotomy. Another minute, which seemed like an hour, ensued. The man was so upset that he was sweating. His olive-colored skin turned red on his face.

The officer listened, and as he listened, he began to write out tickets. In retrospect, I found it interesting that he had not yet asked the man for his driver's license, registration, or insurance. The officer was so convinced, based upon not only the man's driving but also his rude behavior, that the gentleman was going to get tickets that he began to fill them out. All he would have left to do was fill in the man's personal information. The verdict had already been passed, based on the officer's authority.

When the gentleman stopped complaining, all that the officer said was: "May I please have your license and registration?"

Then, it got even better. The gentleman did not have his license with him or any proof of registration. Of course, he expressed this quite vocally. The officer asked him his first and last names, told him to sit tight, and went back to his patrol car. Apparently he could use his computer to retrieve all the information necessary to fill out the tickets.

Upon returning to the car, the officer said, "Sir, you have two options. You can accept these tickets and not get upset, or if you get upset, we can tow your car and you can ride with me to the station. Which will it be?"

I am not sure, but at this point, I thought I saw smoke coming from the man's ears and his eyes bulging like something out of a 1960s cartoon. The veins in his neck were pulsating with the same thud as a teenager's stereo with a subwoofer mounted in the trunk. Yet, surprisingly, the man said nothing.

The officer asked him if he understood the ticket. Still silent, still steaming, the man shook his head. He knew the officer meant business. The officer informed him that although they were on the side of the road, it was inappropriate to block traffic because this was an emergency lane. The officer directed traffic until both the gentleman's car and his own could fit comfortably behind the rest of traffic. From there, the officer monitored the gentleman, following closely behind him as traffic began to move slowly.

This story represents communicating with both conviction and authority. The officer spoke very few words and was very young, yet he had authority. He represented not just the law but also the safety of the people around him. He represented public safety and maintaining the code of law for all of our benefit.

Beyond that, he had conviction, a belief that this gentleman had acted in a way that deserved a ticket. Given the look on the officer's boyish Opie-Taylor face, I have often wondered whether he would have simply given the man a scolding and a warning, if the man had acted in a patient or regretful way. Instead, the gentleman made the officer look foolish. He showed disrespect, and he did not communicate as a leader would. As a result, the officer had conviction that he should give this man a ticket.

This story proves that effective leaders communicate with conviction and authority, based upon their beliefs and what they represent. When we do this respectfully, order is maintained and progress is made. It is only when individuals choose to force conviction and authority to be disciplinary that effective leaders actually use it that way. This officer displayed the conviction that the man should be pulled over and the authority to represent the law. However, the man's inappropriate behavior and actions caused the officer to use that conviction and authority to discipline him with written tickets.

As you look to become a more effective leader, ask yourself what convictions or beliefs you have—and ask yourself what type of authority you wish to communicate. In most situations, your conviction and the authority and confidence with which you speak will open doors of opportunity for others to follow you. I believe this officer acted properly. The gentleman went from being completely irate to mad but silent, based on the conviction and authority this young officer represented. He truly was an effective leader in that situation.

You also have the opportunity to be an effective leader by communicating with conviction and authority. Hopefully, you will not have to deal with irate drivers or other upset individuals. Most of the time, you will not, but we will deal with that type of communication in another chapter. If you speak with polite and humble conviction and authority, you will be amazed at how many individuals will follow you, take your advice, or support your desired outcome. After that, it's up to you to use this responsibility and new level of leadership in a positive manner that benefits everyone.

CHAPTER 14

THE SUPERMODEL WITH A MUSTACHE

TAKING ACTION GIVES US MOMENTUM

Decision and action are two concepts directly connected to the momentum we experience in life. Decision can be viewed as the determination to accomplish something, make something happen, or move to a greater level. Decision by itself is a great dynamic. Decision by itself, however, is not enough.

If that were true, the decision to lose weight would mean that you could drop weight by simply deciding to without changing your current relationship with Little Debbie. But if a decision is going to take root and cause the desired effect, it must produce action. Something must be done. In this scenario, it may mean that you and Little Debbie need some time apart.

Achieving personal excellence, therefore, means doing something. Wanting to achieve personal excellence is not enough. It is a good starting point, but not enough. Deciding to achieve personal excellence is a great next step in that direction, but again, it's not enough. Decision turned into action is what will produce the desired results.

Achieving personal excellence means being a first-rate version of you instead of trying to be a second-rate version of someone else. Too often, individuals try to mimic or copy someone else's behavior in an attempt to get the same type of outcome. While it is admirable to find and follow role models, true personal excellence must come from developing who *you* are to a greater level. You can incorporate or use ideas and concepts from other people. You can adapt certain positive behaviors that they have, but to completely copy or mimic others without first finding out who you are, will not produce the desired effect.

Let me explain it this way: Suppose you were invited to a party or other social gathering. The atmosphere was lively, and people were having fun. But, fun can mean different things to different people. Suppose that one person took fun to mean placing a lampshade on his head and acting silly to make people laugh. That might be fine for him, if he is an extrovert. If you are more of an introvert, you might be the person either laughing at him or with him, or perhaps the person thinking, "Why in the world would he put a lampshade on his head?"

Achieving personal excellence can begin with understanding whether you are naturally an introvert or an extrovert. That is a crucial starting point. For example, I have many friends in various careers. One of my friends is a librarian, and he does well in that field. He has incredible patience for detail, the ability to research until he finds the answer, and the capacity to sit in a very quiet place for a long time. He also can take very calculated actions and is very tolerant of the same routine or activity.

He enjoys coming to the library every day and finds variety not in going to different places, but in researching different materials. He may search the Internet with the same browser at the same computer station (no variety there), but he will be searching for similar yet very different materials. To him, that is all the variety he needs. In fact, he takes joy in the pattern of this routine. He enjoys its predictable nature and does not feel the need to go out and meet new people. Assisting people with their research needs provides him with all the external connection he wants during his workday.

In contrast, I have another friend who is in sales. He tries to be in his office as little as possible. He wants to meet as many people in a day as he can, not just for the sake of making a sale, but for stimuli. His joy comes from constant and steady change in his environment. In fact, some would perceive it as constantly unsteady. It's always something different. Yet, he finds comfort in this atmosphere.

My librarian friend is accustomed to driving the same type of car for a long time. When he buys a different car, it may be the same type of car in a different color, or the same color of car of a different make and model. In other words, something has to be constant and steady for him to feel comfortable. My friend in sales always buys new cars of different makes and models. He often gets bored so quickly with a "lack of something new" that he turns in the car early on its lease to experience something new.

If you put my librarian friend in sales, the constant change and shifting ground would seem overwhelming. He would seem stressed and certainly not enjoy it; he would have no frame or reference point. He is an introvert by nature who likes a controlled, safe, and steady environment.

In contrast, my sales friend finds safety and control in a constantly changing environment because it provides a type of stimuli. If you put him in the role of a librarian, he would no doubt become bored, edgy, and unhappy about missing what he considers stimuli.

The point is this: Each of these people has achieved personal excellence. Christian is an outstanding librarian, while Jim is an outstanding sales professional. Why? Because each of them first analyzed their personality and asked themselves: Am I more an introvert who would like to have constant, familiar surroundings and deal with a relatively continuous group of people? Or am I more an extrovert who would like the stimuli of different people constantly and a fast-paced, rapidly changing atmosphere?

A fast pace can mean something different to each individual. For my librarian friend, "fast-paced" means finding information very quickly for a university student or faculty member, based upon their guidelines. For my friend in sales, "fast-paced" might mean needing to get to the next point quickly to meet with someone whom he has not yet met. But despite their differences, each person started developing his own level of personal excellence by first determining if he was more introvert or extrovert.

I suggest that you ask yourself the same basic question to achieve personal excellence at a higher level. Ask yourself, "What is my actual environment?" That is, where do you feel the most comfortable? Do you picture yourself in a steady environment or a constantly changing environment?

There is no right or wrong answer. This is your journey and your opportunity. As we talk about journey, we would do well to reinforce the point that personal excellence is just that. It is the journey, not the destination. We look back while we are on this journey and see that where we are today has put us in a different position than we were yesterday or last week or last month or last year. It is a journey that begins with decision and is engaged by taking action.

So as we take this action, what does that really mean? Action can be defined, for the purposes of this chapter and this book, as making something happen that causes a positive change. Sure, actions can produce negative changes if they are done without purpose or intent, or if they are done accidentally. But we want to focus first on positive action—those actions in which we purposefully engage, those actions that take us some place other than where we would have gone before.

A great example of this is one of the individuals I just referenced, Jim the salesman. Jim is a phenomenal sales professional. He has honed the art and science of his profession to a level that few achieve. However, he did not start there. He started with a decision that led to action, and that is what produced the results.

Jim grew up on the West Coast. He went to college in the Midwest and majored in history. Jim is a fidgety, fiery, excellent human being. He is approximately 5'10" and weighs just slightly more than a paper clip. For many years he has looked at his frame and told his friends that if he were a female, he could be a supermodel based on how unbelievably, naturally slim he is. He never stops moving, and makes hand motions and gestures constantly. He is pure energy. Even when he sits and listens, he crosses his legs and swings one leg back and forth. It's who he is. It's his personality.

While in college, Jim looked for a career that would give him unlimited opportunity, a chance to excel and make the most of his talents and his abilities. He chose to interview with a life insurance company. That was a decision he made after much contemplation and career investigation. He acted on that by scheduling an interview.

The company, which is very well-known throughout the United States and very highly rated, did not feel that Jim had enough influence on other people or knew enough people of means to be able to be successful in this career. Also, they were interviewing for a position in Chicago. Jim had never lived in Chicago and knew no one there. They quickly dismissed him as someone who didn't know what he would be getting into.

Jim, however, was persistent in his decision and became determined in his action. Following three more interviews, he finally convinced them to give him a chance. The position was commission based and, as he successfully explained to them, they had nothing to lose. Jim was given the opportunity.

After graduation, with less than one-thousand dollars in his pocket, he made the move to Chicago. The irony is that Chicago is called the Windy City. Jim moved there weighing slightly more than a paper clip, and the other agents were certain that, on any given day, they might find him stuck to the side of a newspaper box like a flyer blowing in the wind.

They envisioned themselves kindly peeling him off and shaking him out. As they let go, he would sail down Michigan Avenue or Jefferson Street, smiling and waving with his overcoat flapping in the breeze as he gripped his hat to his head and his briefcase under his arm. On any given windy day in Chicago,

Jim was as apt to fly away as Dorothy's brothers were in her dream of the tornado in *The Wizard of Oz.*

That is a very accurate vision of Jim's career. But it extends much past that. When you look beyond the wonderfully comedic nature of his presence, you see a person who had made a decision to be successful and had taken action many times to make that happen. He moved to Chicago not knowing anyone. He had less than a thousand dollars and needed to pay a security deposit and a month's rent on an apartment, buy insurance for his car, and buy groceries. He needed to be a success very soon—at least enough of a success to pay the bills and eat.

Jim asked himself, "Where would people who need life insurance or disability insurance work—and have the money to buy what they need?" And, "Who wants to spend very little time talking before making their decision to act?" A thought came to him: Chicago is filled with many hospitals. Jim quickly drew up a list of specialty surgeons and other medical professionals, and began making cold calls on these individuals.

Understand that, in the life insurance business, you should come in with two-hundred or so names of individuals you know. Out of every ten names, three will most likely give you an appointment and one will buy. Jim had four-hundred names of individuals who had never heard of him. Yet this wiry young man from the West Coast became a sensation. He became a phenomenal success in the life insurance business and in his company because he continued to act upon his decision, knowing he was an extrovert, liked meeting people, and liked to experience different things.

He took action. I am not over-simplifying his action. He needed to regularly contact more and more of these individuals and ask for referrals. Sometimes, they would give him none. Sometimes, the people would not see him. Sometimes, they would see him but not buy from him. Other times, they would both see him and buy. The sheer volume of appointments, that is, the number of people he saw, enabled him to make a steady income.

Ten years down the road, he and his wife were able to buy a very nice, large home in a historic Chicago neighborhood and provide a private-school education for their daughter. One Christmas, Jim even surprised his wife with a BMW, her dream car.

None of this would have happened if Jim had not made the decision to know his personality and realize that, instead of being in a classroom teaching, he would rather be out visiting with people. He knew his desired outcome, and he took action!

He took an action that initially people laughed at. He didn't know anyone in Chicago. He didn't have friends there with affluence (money to put away and invest), yet he knew that type of people were there. If he made the decision to be successful, his actions would lead him to the right people. His understanding of the "why" enabled him to accomplish the "how."

That brings up another point about achieving personal excellence. It's not always easy, but it is always possible. This book is not a quick-fix solution, but a how-to guide. We are not providing information that everyone can use in the same way, like the answer guide to a test in school. Rather, we're providing some basics upon which you can build a better you, the roadmap for a personal excellence journey. We are not saying there is anything wrong with the way that you are right now. We are assuming that, because you are reading this book, you want to improve yourself continually and experience more of life.

So, what is your starting point? Are you an introvert who would like to hone your skills or perhaps acquire more knowledge and develop yourself that way? Or are you an extrovert who would like to achieve more knowledge in that area? Start by asking yourself who you are, and then together we can go down a pathway, a journey if you will, to develop your skills and abilities consistently on a higher level.

Knowing whether you are an introvert or extrovert can shape your success in life because you will focus on the arena where you want to take action. Many people fail to succeed because they don't take into account their nature and comfort zone. They pick a successful person they would like to be like, read everything about that person, and then act like that person.

That sounds wonderful, right? But what if the person you pick is the opposite of you? Some dream of the extroverted life, but it goes against their very nature. When they try it, their stress level goes through the roof. They are under more stress than others in the same place because they are out of their comfort zone.

As we contemplate this, I would like to ask you to make two decisions: Finish reading this book, and commit to pursuing a better you. Pursue a life that entails not just happiness, but also joy. Commit to finding the things in your life that bring you true and lasting inspiration.

There is a big difference between happiness and joy. Recently, I was on the phone with one of my clients. I am his executive coach. He owns a sales business, and business is slow. He knows that this time will be slow every year, but it makes him unhappy because he likes the excitement and the stimuli of constant change.

He and I began to talk about the difference between happiness and joy, and I saw a lightbulb go on during our conversation. "Steve," I said, "happiness is something that you have on a regular basis, but not in every situation."

"What do you mean?" he said.

I said, "Joy is something that you can take with you because of how you look at the world. Certain situations or circumstances may make you happy or unhappy at the moment, but you will still have joy if you choose to look at the world that way."

"I understand," he said. "I really find joy in my career. I've been in it for many years. However, I get unhappy when the activity level slows down at this time of year."

"I understand," I said.

That's the beauty of understanding the difference between joy and happiness. You can be joyful in any situation. The circumstances may or may not make you happy. When the two align, and you have joy and happiness, that is a time to be remembered so that you can try to duplicate it and make it happen again.

What gives you joy? You can find happiness in many things, but where do you find lasting joy? If happiness and joy were put on a graph, happiness would be the variable that goes up and down, while true joy is the constant that carries you through the down times. Lasting joy must come from inside, from knowing who you are. It must come from knowing where you are now and where you are going, and it must come from understanding your sense of purpose.

Purpose gives life meaning and direction. Purpose gives you an understanding that anything in life can be seen as opportunity. When you understand your purpose, you can fully embrace those things that make you happy. We can even deal with, and not be brought down by, the things that make us temporarily unhappy.

Take time to ask yourself who or what in your life gives you the greatest amount of joy. Is it your spouse? Is it your children? Is it a friend? Who or what gives you joy? Then ask yourself why. Why do you smile when you think of their name—or your house or your car or the vacations you take? Why does that make you smile and give you joy? In other words, what about your personality makes you feel complete or enlightened? Make the decision now to start examining life in that way and to continue to explore personal excellence. When you do, you will be empowered to take actions that will make an immediate difference for the better in your life, so that you can increase the joy and experience life to the fullest.

Think about other people whose decisions and actions have gone far beyond their own personal joy to affect and, in some cases, transform the lives and quality of life of other individuals, including yourself. Thanks, for example, to the decisions and action of Ben Franklin, we have electricity.

Thanks to Thomas Edison, we have light in our homes at night or during storms. We have electricity to power our TVs, our computers, and other electronics.

Thanks to the decision and action of Alexander Graham Bell, we can communicate by telephone any time we choose. And from that technology came our ability to communicate and access information via the Internet.

Thanks to the decision to act by the Wright brothers, we can take a business trip across the country and be home that evening for dinner.

We have more information about current events available moment by moment than ever before. This is thanks in part to a decision to act by individuals like Ted Turner who created CNN, the first all-news channel.

Leaders who make decisions and act do not have to be inventors. They may be like Bill Gates, who did not invent the computer but took the process of developing the software to the level that Microsoft Corporation is today. Thanks to his decision to act, many families have careers there, and users throughout the world can communicate more easily. More than that, his foundation helps people throughout the world—the hungry, the needy, and the poor.

Thanks to the decision to act of individuals such as Mother Teresa of Calcutta, a single person's decision and action has affected many people and set a wonderful example for others as well.

Thanks to the decision to act of Roger Bannister, the first man to run a mile in under four minutes, other individuals have pushed themselves to personal physical and mental excellence, knowing that it could be done.

Thanks to the creativeness of people like Carlile R. Stephens we have Chia Pets. (I just wanted to make sure that you were awake here.)

The point in pursuing excellence is this: You don't need to be like any of the individuals we've used as examples. Don't try to be a second-rate version of any of them—or anyone else. Be a first rate version of you.

Start by understanding yourself and the "why" that drives you. You can tune out all the voices offering suggestions and advice by looking at yourself. No matter what you wear or eat, the basic person is always the same. You cannot run away from yourself to become a better parent, business partner, or whatever.

Listen to your life and body. Are you sleeping poorly, and when was the last time you did something fun? Have you gained weight and can no longer see your feet? Perhaps now is the time to turn decision into action. Change is all around us, so why are we so surprised when we have to change something in our own lives?

This chapter emphasizes two points, neither of which are *Rocket Surgery*, but both of which are important to becoming a star leader. The first is to ask yourself who you are. What drives you? Who and what are important in your life? What do you want out of life? When do you want change to come, and what will that change mean? Ask yourself why you deserve to have more, be more, and do more?

Asking these simple, yet powerful questions will give you the "why," your reason to take action. Taking action for the sake of taking action isn't the point. A dog chasing its own tail is taking action, but it isn't really making progress. You must ask yourself why it is important to take action. Where will it take you? What will it do for you? What will it enable you to be that you aren't now? What will it enable you to have that you don't have now? What will it enable you to do that you aren't doing or experiencing now?

Once you truly understand the "why" at what I call the belly-button level, you have created momentum that will take you as far as your drive and your dreams will allow.

The second point is as simple as the first, but just as powerful in creating momentum. Simply put, take action! Start today. No matter how small a step you take, move toward realizing your dreams. Once you know the "why" behind your action, the action itself will be simple. That does not mean it will always be easy, but you will find a way to make it happen because you are driven by the "why."

Think back to Jim, the human paper clip. He knew the "why" behind his decision to represent that particular life insurance company. He knew the "why" behind his decision to move to Chicago. He knew the "why" behind making the phone calls and setting the appointments. He knew the "why" behind asking the right questions and getting the sale. Knowing all of those "whys" enabled him to phone his prospects, make each appointment, and ask for the sale.

Notice I did not say it was easy to call all those people. I did not say it was easy to get an appointment, and I did not say it was easy to ask for the sale. I only said it was simple. What enabled Jim to do this is his firm understanding of the "whys." He knew why he needed to do what he needed to do. And because he knew, he was able to take action and produce results.

You can do the same thing! No, I don't mean look like a super model with a mustache. No, I don't mean get stuck to a newspaper box by a gust of wind in Chicago. What I mean is to produce results like Jim did by knowing your desired outcome and taking action.

Any of us can do it, if we put our mind to it. Taking action produces a momentum that will continue to build on itself. From the very first action that you take, you will create momentum that will make each succeeding action simpler and easier. You will begin to realize that being a star leader and achieving incredible joy and happiness in life doesn't have to be *Rocket Surgery*. It simply involves decision and action!

CHAPTER 15

DO BALLET SHOES COME IN A 14 EXTRA-WIDE?

ACHIEVING BALANCE IS ESSENTIAL FOR EVERYONE

An often-used and most often misunderstood concept is that people have the ability to "manage their time." Even though it sounds logical, the reality is that it cannot be done. We cannot manage time. We can only manage ourselves. Let me explain.

The term "manage" means to take charge of, influence, or control. Understood in the best possible context, this accurately describes management. Having been a manager of people for many years, and looking at this in a positive context, I'd consider that definition very accurate.

I was put into positions of responsibility and managing other individuals at a young age. Using our definition, I was asked to take charge of them, meaning not just to ensure that they were doing their work, but to make sure they had the necessary tools, education, and emotional and professional support to be successful in their endeavors.

I have always tried to be a positive influence on the people I've managed, not only by providing the things that they needed, but also by being an intentional leader. I have always believed in influencing people with my own actions. I am a firm believer that your own success is the best influence you can have on others. The more successful you are in any area of life, the more positive impact you can have on other people. Finally, I tried to control the environment and the opportunities for them to achieve their best. I gave them every opportunity to succeed. But only rarely did I ever try to control individuals.

The exceptions were on the one or two occasions over the

many years when individuals needed discipline to keep their eye on the target. But most of the time, I didn't try to control individuals but the environment where they worked. Was the workplace positive and upbeat? Did employees have the tools necessary to create and forge positive relationships with clients and prospects? Did they have enough downtime or vacation time? Did I provide them with an adequate budget and schedule enough time for learning opportunities for professional growth? Did I manage myself well enough to have time to be a listening ear, as well as a mentor and coach for their well-being and continued progress?

When we look at managing ourselves and our activities vs. managing time, we can apply the same concept. Time cannot be managed because it is a continuum. If you try to speed up a digital clock or move the hands ahead on an analog clock, you are changing the clock but not actually changing time. Likewise, if you slow down the hands or go backwards on a digital clock, you are changing the clock's display, but you are not managing time. Time cannot be managed. We can only manage ourselves and the events that take place within the context of time. If we understand this concept, it makes more sense to ask if we are "managing ourselves" or "scheduling time," rather than "managing time."

Two examples of this concept come to mind from when I worked in a corporate environment many years ago. The individuals' names were Tom and Steve. I'll describe these two and, as you read through the descriptions, think about the subconscious message each is giving you. The message is most likely accidental, not intentional, but these two individuals still communicated it to those around them.

First, let's catch up with Tom, who worked in the same office and industry as Steve. Tom had been in corporate America but had decided to run his own financial services practice. He voluntarily stepped away from his corporate job, corporate salary, benefits, and company car to pursue the "unlimited opportunity" of owning his own practice with a large, nationally known company. I say "unlimited opportunity" because as this company describes it, your opportunity is limited only by your own abilities or capacities—or, we could say, inability or incapacity.

In our personal excellence seminars, we talk about three principles that will make you stand out over ninety percent of other people. The principles are simple. In fact, in most of our households, our parents taught them to us at a very young age. Opinions differ, but there is a large opinion that much of what we learn about interacting with others in life, we learn between the ages of three and five. The three rules we're usually taught between these ages are:

1. Be on time.
2. Say please and thank you.
3. Do what you say you are going to do.

Tom managed to break all of these rules consistently. He did not mean to; it's just the way he was. Tom often showed up at the office twenty minutes past when the rest of us had agreed to be there every day. He'd rush in, and although he had a nice-looking briefcase and was well dressed, he looked disheveled. This was not because of how his clothes fit, but because of the speed with which he arrived.

One particular morning, we were at our desks setting up our day when the door came swinging open with such speed that it hit the other wall and bounced off the wall guard. Tom came walking in at a very fast pace. He said "Hello" to people when he was already several feet past them, knowing that he was late.

He sat down at his desk in such a fashion that his briefcase knocked over the pile of papers stacked to the right that were backlogged from the past several days of work. He picked up his phone before he took off his suit coat and began retrieving his voice messages, which were piled up from the day before and from when he was supposed to be there that morning.

From several feet over, we could hear him say, "Ugh," and, "Oh no! I forgot all about that!" or, "Oh no! I need to get that in!" He could see his day piling up ahead of him before he even got out of the gate. Then he began to make a series of phone calls.

"Hello, this is Tom. Can I speak to Harry?"

"Hi, Harry. This is Tom. Listen, we have an appointment today at 2:00; I just wanted to let you know I'll be about twenty minutes late. Is that okay? Great. I'll be there as soon as I can, sometime around twenty minutes after. Thanks. I'll see you then."

He made a series of phone calls, four or five in a row, indicating the same type of thing, that he would be about twenty or thirty minutes late. He never asked to confirm the meeting; he sounded hurried and disheveled on the phone and consistently made sure that everyone was aware of this.

After the last phone call, we heard, "Oh shoot!" coming from his office as he realized he was late to meet with the rest of the group. He met with us in our customary weekly meeting to report our figures, forecasts, and projections as to where our personal business was going to go. It was a mutual-accountability group agreed on by individuals who represented the company.

When we began to make our reports, Tom clearly could not find his. As we went around the table, different people gave their statistics, results, and appointment outcomes. Tom still could not find his. When we got to Tom, he looked hurried and then confused. This was followed by a blushing look as he said, "I'm sorry, everyone. I have no idea where my report is. I thought that I put it in here."

He then tried to summarize in a general fashion what his report might have contained. He did his best and, quite frankly, did a relatively adequate job of summarizing his appointments, meetings, and sales calls without having the report in front of him.

After the last person finished, it was time for me to speak as the group leader. "Tom?" I inquired.

"Yes," he said, with the confidence of a fourth-grader who

had left his jelly-smeared spelling test on the counter at home.

"I think it's great that you were able to announce your figures. However, looking back on my notes, I see this is the fifth week in a row where you made projections and fell drastically short of those numbers. Two weeks ago, I encouraged you to adjust your projections to be more accurate or to change something about your actions to be able to meet what you shared with us, namely your goals."

"I understand that I said I'd do that," he replied, "but many things came up along the way, things that I could not predict, things that just, well…happened. Next week, I think I'll be on track. In fact, next week I'll be able to catch up on the previous weeks, in addition to this week."

I raised my eyebrow in disbelief. "Tom, if you have not been able to meet your numbers in the past five weeks, what makes you think week seven will produce those week's, plus this week's agenda, in addition to the goals for this upcoming week?"

"I just have a good feeling about it," he said, folding his arms over his briefcase, which was on top of the table, covering his last week's paperwork. He looked around in an uneasy, half-smiling fashion. I don't think even he truly believed it, but he didn't want to make himself look any more foolish in front of the group.

Next week came. Tom, once again, could not find his report for the week, but he had found the previous week's report. He once again reported to us with relative accuracy, without having the paperwork in front of him, what his week's goals were like. Once again, he fell short. Once again, he projected to catch up.

As we left the meeting that week, none of us had full confidence that he could do it, but we appreciated his blind optimism and his happy-go-lucky nature. Even so, I don't think any of us would have done business with him if we were his clients, based on how he communicated and his lack of delivery.

In contrast, Steve was also in those meetings. Steve would arrive at work on time and sometimes even earlier. In fact, he began a ritual a couple of months into our time together where he would arrive approximately forty-five minutes early to be able to read a book on finance, sales, self-improvement, or some other topic.

I asked him about this one day.

"Steve? I find it interesting that you always seem to be here earlier than the rest of the people I manage."

"I have to get my day set up," he said.

I looked at his desk. Books were tidy and stacked up. Reports were categorized and filed. There were a lot of white space and open areas on his desk. The voice-mail button on his phone was not flashing, indicating that he had already handled waiting voice mails. His open calendar displayed the number of appointments necessary to keep his practice thriving.

"What are you reading?" I asked.

"*Seeds of Greatness* by Denis Waitley," he said.

"Oh, I read that several years ago," I replied. "That's a great book. You'll thoroughly enjoy it."

"Oh, I already have enjoyed it. I read it the first year it came out and again a couple years ago. I've highlighted the parts I want to skim over so I don't have to take the time to read the whole book. I can simply refresh myself on the main points that help me in my practice."

Very efficient, I thought to myself, being impressed.

He then held up another book. "Next week, I'm going to review *Awaken the Giant Within* by Anthony Robbins. I've done the same thing here since it's a thick book. I figured that in just a day or two, I could capture the main points that stuck out to me many years ago when I read it for the first time."

"How does your day look?" I asked, not wanting to take much of his time and appreciating the attention to detail in his schedule.

"My day looks great!" he said. "In fact, I was supposed to have three appointments, according to my voice mail, but two more people who had to reschedule from last week can see me today. Five appointments: It's going to be a full day. I feel great!" he said.

Sometime later, we were back in the conference room for our weekly meeting. As we went around the room, Steve sat to the right of Tom. Since we went in a counterclockwise fashion, following Tom's disheveled and unorganized report (falling short of his goals but promising to do better next week), we came to Steve. Steve's report, posture, and communication were very different from Tom's. He sat in a confident fashion. He made great eye contact and spoke with the authority of one who stood behind his figures and statistics. He reported to us that he was somewhat frustrated but generally happy.

"Why the frustration?" I asked.

"I don't think I'm setting my goals high enough," he said.

"You're one of the group's leaders," I replied with confidence. The rest of the group nodded in assurance.

Steve said, "Yes, but each week, I don't meet my goals—I beat them."

"What's the problem?" another group member asked.

"I don't know if I'm setting my goals high enough," he said.

"Great point," I replied. "What would you like to do about that?"

"I'd like to take it up incrementally, week-by-week. If I fall drastically short," he said, "then I'll know I've stretched too far. If I meet those, I can push myself a little more."

This didn't surprise me. It was indicative of someone who had read self-improvement books and continued to review them on a regular basis outside of his working time.

"That's a great idea!" said Tom in complete disbelief, as if he had not been able to think of that several weeks earlier. He took out a piece of paper to write it down but couldn't find a pen.

He borrowed one from Steve.

Internally, I rolled my eyes and shook my head. Outside, I just smiled and complimented Tom for picking up on the idea. Steve said nothing and smiled as he handed him the pen.

As we left the meeting, we were all on schedule. Tom was so impressed by Steve that he stopped him on the way out the door.

"Steve, do you have a moment?" he said.

"Not really, Tom. I have to go. I have an appointment I have to get to."

"Where is it?" he asked.

"On Franklin and Adams Street. I have to be there in thirty minutes."

"That'll only take you fifteen; we have plenty of time. I just need to ask you a few things," Tom continued, ignoring Steve's comments.

"I really can't, Tom," Steve said.

"But you have thirty minutes to get to an appointment that is only fifteen minutes away," said Tom.

"True," said Steve, "but I like to get there early and be prepared. Also, I like to review my forms just before I walk into the office so that I can be familiar with their personal information. It also gives me a fifteen-minute buffer zone in case anything happens or the train's running late. I can be available at 4:30 today," Steve said. "I'll answer any questions you have then."

"Sounds great," said Tom.

Tom and Steve left. I could almost predict what the afternoon would bring. At 4:25, Steve arrived at the office to close out his reports, stack up his paperwork, send his assistant the paperwork for the next day, and retrieve any phone messages he had. 4:30 came; 4:30 went. 4:40 came; 4:40 went. 4:50 came, and Steve was still doing his paperwork, not wanting to waste any time or idly wait for Tom.

At 4:55, Tom came hurriedly through the front door. "I'm sorry I'm late," he said, looking somewhat sweaty and out of breath. "How are we on time?" he said with a smile that asked for approval.

"I'm sorry," said Steve, "I've got a 5:30 that I have to be at with my son. I have to leave here in five minutes."

"Great. I'll be right back, and we can go over the questions," said Tom.

Steve agreed, but in disbelief began to pack his bags.

At 5:00, Tom came around the corner. "Okay, I've got the paperwork," he said.

"Tom, I'm sorry," replied Steve. "I simply can't stay. I have an appointment. I'll tell you what; lay the questions on my desk. I'll look at them first thing in the morning when I get in, before I start my reading time. If I have time—which I'm sure I will—I'll answer them for you any way I can."

Tom agreed and once again apologized for not being able to find the forms he was going to ask the questions from. The next morning, Steve arrived at the office at his usual time, book in hand. He set up his display and did his usual routine of picking up his paperwork, which had been completed the day before by his assistant, and getting his voice mails. He looked at his desk; there was no paperwork from Tom. Not at all surprised, he started his work day.

Even though you may not know the real people in this example, we all know people like them. How many Toms do you know in your life? How many Steves do you know? And what did Tom in this story tell you? What did Steve tell you? Are you a Steve or a Tom?

In my life, I know some Toms, but I try to limit my interactions with them and the amount of reliance I place on them. Quite frankly, they usually do not come through. They are trying to manage time rather than manage themselves, and that does not work very well, as we said earlier in this chapter.

I know a lot of Steves. Quite frankly, I am a Steve, even though I have a different first name, and I surround myself with as many Steves as I can in my personal and professional life.

Why do I try to surround myself with Steves instead of Toms? The answer is simple. Steves understand the concept of achieving balance. They balance out their schedules and manage themselves in the process.

Steve is not a better person than Tom. I know them both very well, and they are both great guys. Tom, however, has never grasped the concept that you cannot manage time. He is constantly striving to experience the results of Steve, but he can't ever seem to do so because he has not mastered the concept of achieving balance.

When they worked together, Tom lived by the clock rather than by his priorities. He never got as far as breaking down necessary tasks, supporting tasks, and fun tasks. As a result, he was barely able to complete the necessary ones. The supporting tasks never seemed to get done. Fun tasks were not even on his radar screen.

In contrast, Steve completed the necessary tasks first. He did so in order and then built in time around them for supporting tasks, such as reading the books by Denis Waitley or Anthony Robbins. When he was away from work, you got his voice mail because he was having fun with his family and friends. In other words, first, he completed what was necessary. Second, he positioned himself for continued growth. Finally, he made sure that he had fun away from work.

The point of this chapter is simple. Don't try to manage time. Instead, try to manage yourself. If you successfully manage yourself, rather than trying to manage time, you can begin to experience the type of consistent results that Steve does. In addition, you will experience the kind of consistent upward growth that Steve enjoys.

I have mentioned that Steve was re-reading the Denis Waitley and Anthony Robbins books. On a regular basis, I would check for fun to see what he was reading. It was always about self-improvement, self-growth, the marketplace, or something else to help him be a better person. Often it was a book he had not read before, but sometimes it was a book he was reviewing to revisit the main points for greater results.

What about you? Are you surrounding yourself with positive things that will help you to see life better, to see yourself better?

Are you taking enough downtime or vacation time? I list those as two separate things. You can take downtime daily by exercising in the gym, playing with your children, taking a walk with your spouse, taking a walk by yourself with a cup of coffee downtown during lunch hour, or anything else. Vacation time is a set period of time—days or weeks—away from work where you can get refreshed and reflect on how successful you have been in different areas and what you can do to replicate that going forward.

Have you given yourself an adequate budget of time and resources to accomplish the things that you want so that you aren't hurried and don't feel overwhelmed? If you feel overwhelmed or are always behind on your bills, you are trying to work too much, and maybe you are trying to live beyond your means. If you feel that you never get enough work done, perhaps you are not prioritizing, or quite frankly, you are trying to do too much.

As funny as it sounds, are you a listening ear to yourself? Do you ever sit back and ask yourself how you communicate with other people? Is it in a hurried and disheveled fashion or a self-confident and productive way? What are they hearing you say and seeing you do? Intentional communication is much more powerful than unintentional.

Finally, have you surrounded yourself with coaches and mentors who help get you on track and keep you on track? Many individuals hire me on a regular basis for periods of time—a quarter, a half-year, or year—to keep them on track and to help them stay focused on what they have told me is important. Have you surrounded yourself with people who can be your coaches or mentors?

As we've said, this book is called *It's Not Rocket Surgery* because the journey to personal excellence is not really complicated. Doing what we need to do to pursue personal excellence and balance our schedule does not necessarily mean trying to manage time. It means managing ourselves.

Take a look at your day today as you read—or perhaps

yesterday or the past day or two. Ask yourself three things:

1. Am I communicating to others in a confident and controlled fashion?
2. Am I doing those things that will allow me to get where I want to be in a timely manner?
3. Am I taking time to make sure that I stay refreshed and relaxed on this journey of personal excellence?

In answering these short but powerful questions about your own life, you are continuing your journey of personal excellence at a great pace. You are also doing something that will prove invaluable to you. You are not trying to manage time, but yourself.

The title of this chapter asks if they make size 14 ballet shoes for a reason. While I have never taken ballet (and don't suspect I would look good in pink tights and a tutu), I know that it takes balance. Anyone at almost any age, young or old, can learn the principles of physical balance through ballet instruction.

The same thing holds true in our lives. Any of us, regardless of our age or experience, can begin to make dramatic and powerful advances in balancing our lives by taking the first step. And that first step is very simple: Just focus on what you can control.

When you focus on what you cannot control, you are out of control. When you focus on what you can control, you are in control. Begin today to direct your energies to focusing on what you can control. I guarantee that four things will happen:

1. You will feel more in control.
2. You will feel less stress.
3. You will be more effective.
4. You will be more productive.

As you continue to do this day after day, you will build

productive momentum. Focusing on what you can control will become more and more natural. It will be easier to diminish, and ultimately eliminate, all negative stress. You will become more and more effective because your mind will find new and better ways to do things.

In just a short time, achieving balance will come naturally to you. As you see the results of your new approach, your mind will literally develop pathways to increase the positive effects you are experiencing. In turn, your intentional leadership skills will attract others to you. You will begin to experience a level of living that will make you ask yourself, "Why didn't I do this before?"

The exciting news is that you can start today! No matter how much you are like Tom or Steve, you can begin your journey of increased life balance today. All it takes is the decision to focus on what you can control. Enjoy the journey! It will take you to amazing places!

Chapter 16

Good Things Come In Threes

Three Resources We Must Master To Become Star Leaders

A resource, by definition, is a thing, idea, or person—or more than one of any of these—that can help us accomplish our goals and achieve our outcomes. We have all been given resources, some more than others. But each of us has the same three basic ones, whether we attended a private upper-class school or an under-funded urban school and whether we have been promoted to president or made chief maintenance engineer. These resources are ours to use, however we choose. *Star leaders have learned how to master these three critical resources*:

1. Time.
2. People.
3. Money.

Each of us has to decide whether we are going to use these resources wisely or waste them. And our choices will make a tremendous difference in our journey toward personal excellence.

Leaders of workshops and sales training and company development programs often ask the participants to list the resources at their disposal. The leader will say, "On a piece of paper, list the resources—time, people, and money—that you have to help you reach your goals."

Then the leader will ask, "Are you using all of these? Do not stop writing until you have every resource on your list." The purpose behind this exercise is to get participants thinking about the many resources available so that they truly see their possibilities.

After this, the instructor will say, "Go through your list, and ask yourself how many of these resources you are currently using." If you are like me, this is an "Aha!" moment. When I first did this exercise, I realized how many resources were right in front of me that I was not using as an effective leader.

When you do this exercise, you inevitably realize that you are not using enough of your resources. Julie remembers how, when she was a girl, the Girl Scouts used the "buddy system." The idea was to always go with a buddy so that if one person was weaker or needed help, someone else was always there.

You can do the same thing as you consider your resources. Start by selecting one person from your list who will make a great "buddy for progress." Bounce ideas off each other, learn from each other, and give open and honest feedback. Girl Scout buddies are primarily for safety reasons in the outdoors, but I cannot think of a more dangerous environment than the corporate world.

As you begin to examine your resources, start with the immediate. Examine the time you have, the people in your inner circles, and the other resources that you have. Then begin to expand those circles. Start to be creative, and examine the time that you could be using to make progress that you currently aren't. Think of the people with whom you might not be in contact but that perhaps you should invite into your inner circles. Finally, think about the money that you spend on things that don't have a great rate of return and how you could instead be investing that into something with a great rate of return.

As we have said several times throughout this book, asking "how" rarely gives the answer you need to make significant progress in life. Asking "why" gets at the heart of the matter. Before you ask yourself how you can find more time, engage more individuals, or get a better bang for your buck, ask yourself why you would do that.

The "why" is going to give you the vision and drive to

discover the "how." The "why" gives us a reason for decision and a reason to take action. Asking "why" gives meaning and substance to literally every decision we make. "Why" gives the underlying drive to our actions. And when we understand the "why," the "how" follows logically and often quite easily. Understanding why we do things also inspires creativity. It gives an added spark. It allows us to take ownership of the process. It empowers us to have conviction in our actions, and it invites us to enjoy the process.

Classes that teach us to examine our resources often break them down into so many categories that many people find the process overwhelming. As a result, they simply give up. I have been through seven different sales and personal development schools that taught this "how to" formula. In each case, I found the approach admirable but not very efficient or effective. I could see where the writer of the course was coming from, in a textbook sense. However, as is often the case, there is a tremendous difference between "textbook" and "real-life practical application."

In contrast to this, Julie and I studied how the most effective leaders engaged in personal excellence. What we found, in every case, was that they did not try to over-analyze their resources. They did quite the opposite. They simply divided them into three main categories: time, people, and money. This freed them from thinking about the "how" and empowered them to think about the "why."

When they did this, they found that, rather than being a chore, the process became an exciting journey. This journey of personal excellence led them to begin leading lives of more effective leadership. *Effective leaders efficiently and effectively use the resources they have at their disposal.* And they do this at an increasingly higher level. Why? Because, in this case, repetition increases efficiency. Let's take a closer look at each of the three categories these leaders use.

Time: Compare, Experience, and Predict

Time can be understood very simply as past, present, or future. While these categories are simple, each is an important dynamic. If we briefly examine each one, we will see how effective leaders understand them.

Effective leaders learn from the past. They do not dwell on the past or live in it. Effective leaders quickly categorize past events as negative or positive. If an event was negative, they ask themselves why it took place. When they understand the "why," the "how" becomes obvious. They ask themselves how this can be avoided in the future. In this way, the negative outcome is turned into a positive learning experience.

If an event was positive, they ask themselves why, much as they did with the negative, but from a different perspective. They ask themselves why to understand how they can replicate this in the future. Was this a success because of something they did? If so, they can try to do that again. Did it succeed because of something that someone else did? If so, they can commend and encourage that behavior or encourage other individuals and lead them in the same direction.

Effective leaders live in the present. Effective leaders understand that progress is never in past tense or future tense. It is always in present tense. In other words, we are always moving backward or forward in our progress. Effective leaders don't live in the past, but they compare the outcomes of the present to those of the past.

Effective leaders are always trying to make today a better experience than yesterday. They are always seeking to grow and to lead others to grow. In doing so, they carry into the present only those thoughts, words, and actions that produced positive results. They look to discard any thoughts, words, and actions that may have held themselves or others back.

Effective leaders look to the future. While effective leaders live in the present, they are always asking themselves how actions and interactions today will affect future outcomes. They do not see the present as an isolated time in their lives. They see it as part of a continuum and as a pathway for greater progress tomorrow. They return again to the "why:" Why would I want to build relationships with certain individuals? Why would I want to act and react in a certain way? Why would I want to incorporate a particular idea, dynamic, or way of doing things? They do this with an eye on the present and a big-picture view of the future.

If we understand time in these three capacities, we can see it as a valuable resource to be learned from, experienced, and used to look ahead. To apply this concept, effective leaders compare, experience, and predict.

They compare to the past. They ask: Did this action produce positive results? Did this person prove trustworthy in past interactions? Did this situation put me in a less advantageous or more advantageous position?

They experience the present. They ask: Is this producing the results I desired or expected? Is this person someone with whom I want to build a relationship, and for what purpose? Will saying a certain thing or doing a certain thing now produce the outcome that I want?

They predict the future. By this, we do not mean some sort of magical prediction. Rather, effective leaders connect cause and effect. They connect action and outcome. They ask: What would I need to say or do today to get the outcome I want tomorrow? Who and what do I want in my future? What step can I take today to get closer to having the future I want?

Money: Having More to Do and Be More

Effective leaders look at money in much the same way. They do not see money as stationary or set at its present value. Rather, effective leaders see money as a means. In doing so, they view it as either decreasing or increasing their ability to be, have or do. As a resource, money can allow them to have more free time and to be more adventurous on vacations, more generous with their donations, more respected in certain circles, or more influential.

For an increase in any of these areas, effective leaders need to increase the amount of money they earn, have, or invest. Increasing their earnings means being of more value to those who sign their paycheck (if they are employees), or those who buy their product or service (if they are entrepreneurs). Increasing what they have means being a better saver instead of a spender. This means paying themselves first.

Increasing their investments means understanding the concept of time and learning where the company or fund in which they are investing has been, is, and will be. The more they can increase any of these areas by using money more effectively, the more that they can be, have, or do. And by doing so, they show that they truly understand money as a resource.

When Julie and I give personal excellence seminars, we identify money as a resource that can be divided three ways:

1. Part of it is yours for later.
2. Part of it is to share.
3. Part of it is for now.

Individuals who have effectively gone down the path of personal excellence and become star leaders have clearly understood this. Let's take a closer look at each of these.

Part of the money you earn is yours for later. Take a percentage of what you earn, and save it! Put it in a savings account or a retirement account where you will not spend it now, but it will be there for a rainy day later on. Whatever percentage is right for you is the right percentage to save.

You can start today, even with a dollar. Just take a dollar out of your wallet and put it in an envelope marked "Savings." The fact that it is only a dollar is not important. Don't get hung up on that. What's important is understanding the concept and the power of discipline. Try this for thirty days, then for forty-five days, then for ninety. Remember, it takes thirty days to make a habit. It takes forty-five days to make a routine, and it takes ninety days to make a lifestyle.

Give a percentage of what you earn to those less fortunate and in need. This giving can be through your church or through civic or community organizations. It may be directly through an individual you know or through any other charity or individuals that you feel are less fortunate than you are. Julie and I practice this through giving to our church. We give away a part of everything we make, and we also have helped the less fortunate through groups like Rotary International. There are many ways, but part of the money you earn can give you fulfillment as you help others in need.

Part of what you earn is yours to use now. Use some of your money to help improve your life now. Use it wisely, and you will enjoy it more and have more to use. Enjoy that portion now. You have most likely worked very hard for it.

People: Power in Numbers

Effective leaders see people as a resource because they understand the power of numbers. A group always has more power than one person alone. Effective leaders understand that without people, they would not be leaders but sole entities. Sole entities have much less opportunity and fewer successes in life than teams. Effective leaders are always asking themselves the following questions about people:

- "Do I want this person on my team?"
- "Do I want to be on this person's team?"
- "What can he or she bring or add to my team?"
- "What can we accomplish by joining forces?"
- "What skills and abilities does he or she have that I don't?"
- "What relationships does this person have or could he or she develop?"
- "What could we accomplish together?"

Effective leaders see people and relationships as precious resources, not disposable ones. We tend not to take care of things we consider disposable, for logical reasons. When it comes to people, this attitude can have a high price. Companies that think this way lose trained people and then have to spend the time and money to start over with a new person.

A company with a high turnover rate might as well tell its competitors, "No really. I insist that you go first. You have highly trained people who are treated right and stay working for you. Go find your next client while we go back to ground zero and train yet another employee."

When something is precious, we take care of it and see it as something to be cherished and protected. Effective leaders view people and relationships this way. They see people as important resources on the journey of life. They recognize that even though there are millions of people in this world and they will encounter thousands during their lifetime, each one is unique. This uniqueness makes them special and valuable.

When we pursue the path of personal excellence, we cannot separate this resource of people from the other two resources of time and money. In fact, we have to overlap this resource with the other two. This is done by asking two simple and straightforward questions: "How much time do I wish to spend with this person and to what end?" and, "How much is this relationship worth to me and why?"

These questions are not asked out of selfish gain but to make the most of our resources and our opportunities. All of us know certain people that we don't want to—and shouldn't—spend much time with. Why? Because their actions, outlook, and behaviors are not positive—but negative. Their interactions are not uplifting—but selfish and destructive.

These are not the people we want to spend our time with, and they are not the kind of people we want to consider in this chapter. You know you have found one when he or she cries over the rain and thinks it will stop. They are the two-year-olds trapped in adult bodies that still throw fits and think people will change because of them.

Instead, we want to focus on people from whom we can learn and who can help us grow. We want to focus on people who see the good in themselves and their situation, the good in us, and the good in life. When we focus on these people, we see our relationships as investments. We are investing time and energy into these relationships so that we can all benefit and produce positive results. Effective leaders see this as a continuum. They consistently and constantly seek out and build relationships with people who see, understand, and reflect the positive things in life.

I can think of a great example of someone who did not understand these three categories of resources and who missed many opportunities as a result.

When I was in graduate school, I attended school with Dan. He was a great guy who was very excited to be embarking on a second career. He had been successful at his first career but felt a calling to enter a different kind of work. He meant well, loved his wife and family, and was kind to his friends, but he clearly did not understand his resources.

Whenever we saw Dan or heard his name, another classmate and I would turn to each other and quietly joke, "There's just no time! There's not enough time!"

That is how Dan saw life. Nothing seemed to get done on time, because there simply was not enough of it. Dan always worked at his own pace, doing things his way, and then turning to the next task. I often felt that when he began a project, time ceased to exist—or at least it stood still. Deadlines meant nothing to him, and he became sidetracked easily by things that entertained or educated him but had nothing to do with the project at hand.

Dan was intelligent enough to be a top student, but he only had average to above-average grades. That's because he was docked constantly for turning in papers that were either late or unacceptable, based on graduate school standards. If a paper was not accepted, he would have to do exceptionally well on another exam or paper to get a passing grade. Whenever anyone commented on this or tried to encourage him, his reply was, "There is just not enough time! There is just not enough time!"

In contrast to Dan, I also went to graduate school with Ed. Much like Dan, Ed was a great guy. However, Ed always seemed to have enough time for his projects, his studies, his friends, and his personal time.

What I found interesting was that both Dan and Ed had twenty-four hours in a day to work with. Both slept around eight hours a night, but Dan never had enough time to do the same assignments that Ed completed (well and on time) for our professors.

The difference may have been what they chose to do. Dan did a tremendous amount of socializing in graduate school during time when Ed was perhaps in the library or cutting his socializing short to spend time on the paper or task at hand. They both had enough time, but Ed chose to see time as a resource.

Dan would mark on the calendar when a paper was due, and the closer it got to the due date, the more pressure he would feel to buckle down, which seemed an almost impossible task for him. In contrast to that, Ed had learned to count backwards the number of days that he had on a project. For example, if he was assigned a paper that was due in forty-five days, Ed would write a forty-five in his notebook. The next day, Ed would write a forty-four. The next day he would write a forty-three, and so on. That way, Ed felt the pressure early to start using his resource of time so that if anything unexpected happened, he had used this resource well.

Many things crept up at the last moment and prevented Dan from meeting his deadlines. Ed had unexpected events take place as well, although for some reason, not as many as Dan. But because Ed had started earlier, he was able to complete the project in the time he had left. It was amazing how much lower Ed's stress was than Dan's. And it is amazing what one can accomplish in just a few minutes a day on a project, once it has been broken down into manageable pieces.

Another thing that characterized Dan was a lack of money. When we wanted to go out to eat, see a movie, or do something else in our free time, he never had enough money. He didn't have exorbitant medical bills or unforeseen expenses; he simply did not know how to manage his resource of money. He would end up paying more by waiting until the last minute on things such as late fees for overdue bills, or last-minute class registration.

Keep in mind that Dan was fifteen years older than Ed. Yet, during the same year that Dan bought a car that was older than his previous one because it was all he could afford, Ed was able to buy his fiancé a sports car for her 21st birthday. Dan had had more earning years than Ed, but he had not used his resources well. He saw money as something fluid that came in one hand and went out the other. Ed saw money as a resource, something he could use wisely and in sparing amounts.

When we left school, Dan had significant debt and an older car. Ed had a much smaller debt, and his fiancé had a newer sports car. Ed saw money as a resource to get where he wanted to go and used it accordingly. Dan did not.

Dan and Ed also differed in how they used the resource of people. When they were assigned a paper or a topic, particularly by one professor, they each went about the task entirely differently. Dan would write down when the paper was due and then not think about it for a week or two, or more.

By the time he went to the library to check out the appropriate books, they had already been checked out, and he was scrambling to find the necessary information. (This was several years ago when you could not simply jump on the Internet to find an answer.) Dan would then scramble to find anyone on campus who had the book he needed, or he would call someone who lived off campus and drive across town to their house, sometimes to find out that it was not the right book at all.

In contrast, when a paper or project was assigned, Ed immediately pulled together a group of individuals, each of whom would take part of what we were assigned and tackle that individually. The group would meet regularly to share what they had learned with each other. They would also check out the appropriate books on the day the project was assigned, or put a hold on any book that was checked out and grab it as soon as it came back in. This is probably why Dan could never find the books he needed. Ed and the others in his group would exchange books as they needed to reference things. Long before the paper was due, they would have it done.

What was the difference between Dan and Ed? It was more than just the use of time and money. *Ed engaged people in the process.* Following graduate school, Ed moved into a senior leadership position. In fact, he was the youngest representative of a billion-dollar international foundation. He wasn't chosen for the job because he was a child prodigy or a genius, but because he knew how to use resources and lead a team.

Working as a team, his group accomplished far more than any of them would have on their own, and in a timely fashion. This saved the foundation a tremendous amount of money, and they were all able to benefit individually as well. Ed was the youngest producer, manager, and then trainer that the foundation had ever had—and he set some national sales records.

The last I heard, Dan was still struggling with seeing time, money, and people as resources. As a result, he has continued to struggle with his career, and he remains very frustrated in his personal life. Both he and Ed were given the same resources, but Dan burned through his at a faster and faster rate.

We all know people like Dan and Ed. When you look in the mirror, decide that today you will look differently at your time, your finances, and the people in your life. That will empower you to build on these opportunities each new day and bring you closer and closer to your goals.

Let's summarize the points we have covered in this chapter.

Do you see time as a resource to maximize your happiness and the happiness of others? Do you see time as a gift that you must use today? According to an old saying, *"Time is given to you today. You cannot keep it; you must spend it or invest it accordingly."* How will you choose to invest your time today to provide a better life for tomorrow? And what can you do today to make tomorrow better for you and those you care about?

Do you see money as a resource to help you reach the outcomes you want? Do you see it as a way to build the future you want and to enjoy the fulfillment of helping others who are less fortunate?

And do you see people as the strongest asset in your life? Consider this: *Companies don't exist in reality. They only exist on paper for legal purposes. In reality, companies are made up of entities called people.*

Relationships are key to being a successful leader. When you see individuals as a resource, you will contribute back to them. Together, the tide will rise, and you will become a star leader leading them on the continuing journey of personal excellence!

CHAPTER 17

BREAK OUT THE LEG WARMERS

TAKING TIME FOR YOU ENABLES YOU TO TAKE TIME FOR OTHERS

In the midst of writing this book, Julie and I left the snow-covered landscape of Wisconsin to expand our opportunity to serve. This opportunity presented itself in the breathtaking warmness of Chattanooga, Tennessee. Shortly after moving here, I signed Julie and myself up for a yearlong membership at a local health club. Within two days of living here, I went to the gym for my first workout.

I found the locker room and changed for my workout. The club was both new to us and new in general, as it had just been built. It had that crisp, clean, "someone work up a sweat in me" feel. It is a beautiful facility with full basketball courts, a suspended running track, weight rooms, aerobic rooms, cardio equipment, a café, booths, and all the other amenities that you can imagine. I took a deep breath of air, smiled at my new fitness center, and headed to the cardio room.

As I walked in, my first reaction was, "Yipes!"

The room was beautiful and state of the art. It had an air-supported floor, stair steppers, elliptical machines, treadmills, and exercise bikes. There, on the first stair stepper was Becky. Becky was my "Yipes!"

She smiled and said, "Hi! Are you here to work out?"

No, I thought in comedic sarcasm, *I always dress this way for business meetings.* I was wearing a pair of white Nikes, red basketball-length shorts, and a blue t-shirt with a large "Superman" logo on the front. Hey, give me a break; mental attitude rules the day.

"I sure am," I said as I somewhat reluctantly got onto the stair stepper next to her.

"I'm Becky!" she said in a friendly manner. "And you are?" she asked.

Blinded by the variety of colors you're wearing, I thought to myself.

"I'm Chris," I said in a friendly, open tone.

"Great facility, huh?" she added.

"It sure is," I agreed. "My wife and I just joined it yesterday. Today is my first official workout," I proudly offered.

"You'll love it!" she commented while catching her breath.

"I am sure we will," I readily agreed.

Becky was in her mid-fifties and was wearing a pair of beige, soft-leather Reebok aerobic shoes that were quite "in" when I was in college in 1985. She had on lavender tights and bright purple, fuzzy legwarmers that I am sure she purchased the same year as the Reeboks, if not before. She had on a one-piece workout body suit that was quite possibly lifted from the former set of the *Mork and Mindy* sitcom of the 1970s...it was rainbow colored. She also had a matching rainbow-colored headband that pushed her perm straight up toward the ceiling.

Her pushed-up, permed bangs flopped up and down in rhythmic motion as she vigorously kept pace with the music playing on the television. She wiped her forehead with the back of her wrist, which was covered with a bright purple, fuzzy sweatband that matched her legwarmers.

"I just started coming in here last week," she said between breaths.

"Really?" I commented. I was a bit shocked. She was out of date by fashion standards, but her ability to be this far into her workout and carry on a conversation suggested that she was in shape. "You just started working out last week?" I said in disbelief.

"Heavens, no," she said half-chuckling through breaths. She continued, "You can only watch Richard Simmons videos so many times before you get bored. If I work out to *Sweatin' to the Oldies* one more time, I think my head will explode," she said emphatically as her bangs rose above and dipped below her rainbow-colored headband.

Don't laugh, I thought to myself. *Just don't laugh.* I couldn't help it. I burst into laughter. "Wowzers! *Sweatin' to the Oldies,* huh?"

"Oh, I know, I know. It sounds funny, and it is funny," she offered in complete honesty. "I started years ago and just kept going and going and going with it."

"Kind of like the Energizer Bunny?" I asked.

"Exactly!" she said, picking up her pace as the machine increased in speed.

"So why the change?" I asked. "*Sweatin' to the Oldies* has been around for quite a while. You must have been doing that for quite some time. Why change right now?" I was genuinely interested in her response.

"I wasn't doing enough for myself," she answered.

"I don't understand," I said with sincere curiosity.

"I was using Richard Simmons' tapes to work out."

"Do you have something against Richard Simmons?" I asked with a grin. "Because if you do, that was apparently a lot of years of tolerance."

"No, not at all," she said, smiling while continuing her brisk pace.

"Oh, I see, kind of built-up resentment over time because he could eat what he wanted to and still look the same each time you replayed the tape, over and over again," I said as I grinned.

"You're quite the comedian, aren't you?" she said as she laughed and wiped her brow.

"I try," I said as I shrugged my shoulders and gave a humble grin.

"Actually," she continued, "it was easy for me to not 'get around' to working out some days because the phone would ring, someone would drop by, or I would see my 'to-do' list and think that I should be working on that instead."

"Ah yes," I offered, "the ever-talking and beckoning project list."

"Well, not talking," she said, smiling, "but definitely beckoning nonetheless. This way, by getting into a separate environment, I am specifically setting the time and energy aside to take care of myself."

"That is a very wise move," I assured her.

"You have to," she declared. "If you don't take care of yourself, don't expect anyone else to take care of you."

"I agree," I said. I fully saw her point. "I would even take it a step further. No pun intended," I said smiling and pointing to the stair stepper.

"Are you quitting your day job any time soon for a stand-up comedy gig?" she inquired.

"Not likely," I assured her. "But seriously, you not only can't expect others to take care of your health, but you can't do what you are supposed to do for them personally or professionally if you are physically or mentally unable to."

"That is a great point!" she exclaimed, increasing her stepping to keep up with the machine's increased speed.

"Thangu, Thangu very much," I said in my worst Elvis Presley impression.

She laughed. "I think that more people need to understand that principle," she said with emphasis as she once again wiped her brow with her purple wristband. "Too many people push themselves hard, which isn't a bad thing. The problem is that they don't give their body or their mind any downtime to recover and recuperate."

"I completely agree," I said. She was speaking my language. "That is what Julie and I have been saying for years."

She added, "What most people don't take time to understand is that it is much easier to prevent illness and burnout if you take it a step at a time. Instead, they push and push and push until finally their body, or their emotions, just give out."

"You are completely right," I said. "I'm a professional speaker and trainer, and one of the speeches I have used is 'Find Your Inner Roger Bannister.' "

"Roger Bannister. The first person to break the four-minute mile," she said, never breaking her stride.

"That's right," I agreed. "He knew how to push himself..."

She jumped in on my sentence and added, "...But he also knew how to train regularly, and he understood the importance of rest."

"Exactly!" I knew she got it.

"So you are a speaker, are you?"

"No, not really, but I play one on TV," I said in my best George Harrison voice. She laughed, and I laughed. "What do you do?" I asked.

"I am a neurosurgeon," she responded.

I burst into laughter.

"I didn't realize it was that funny of a career," she said, genuinely intrigued by my response.

"This is perfect," I said. "Absolutely perfect!"

"Pardon me?" she said, once again with complete confusion.

"My wife, who happens to be my business partner, and I are writing a book on personal excellence and effective leadership. It's called, *It's Not Rocket Surgery: How to be a Star Leader at Every Level.* I'm laughing because at the beginning of the book, I mention a brain surgeon that I met in Wisconsin. Now I meet you, and we're talking about the same issues that are in the book."

"What a coincidence," she exclaimed as intrigued as I was.

"Exactly," I agreed. "That's why I laughed. It is just too coincidental."

"Getting back to what we were discussing," she continued, without missing a beat or being sidetracked in the slightest, "prevention is so much more powerful than rebuilding after burnout. You must take time for yourself. I see that mistake made in my profession all the time. We tend to think that we are doing a service by constantly doing for others and not ourselves."

"Oh, I agree," I said emphatically. "Sacrifice in the name of service, but to a fault."

"That is why I am in here and not with Richard Simmons."

I am not going to touch that with a thirty-nine-and-a-half-foot pole, I thought to myself, recalling the words from the theme song to *How the Grinch Stole Christmas.*

"It is amazing," she said, her pace now slowing to 'cool down' mode as the stair stepper began to slow. "I can come in here completely stressed out and leave completely, or at least mostly, stress-free."

Not fashion conscious, but at least stress-free, I thought to myself. *One out of two isn't bad. To be stressed out and dressed like that is just wrong for so many reasons.* "You know," I added, "there are times that I don't even feel stressed out, but I exercise anyway as a preventive measure, both physically and psychologically. When I leave, I am amazed at how stress-free I feel, even though I didn't think I felt stressed when I came in."

She wrapped her towel around her neck. I winced. Plaid shower towels should never be placed next to rainbow-colored, striped headbands. *She is amazing,* I thought. *She can operate on the human brain, yet she has single-handedly mastered being the walking fashion citation.*

As she stood there cooling down from her workout while I continued mine, she continued our conversation. "Exercise is a great way to take care of yourself, but there are other ways, too. I just wish that more people realized that," she said.

"True. Very, very true," I concluded.

We said our good-byes, and she left the fitness area to hit the showers. After she left, I began to think about the overall topic of taking time for yourself and taking care of yourself.

As I did, I recalled an executive that Julie and I had admired for several years for this very reason. His name was William, but he went by Bill. Bill was a very successful and wealthy man. He worked in downtown Chicago and was the president, chairman, and CEO of a large insurance holding company when we met him. He had three demanding titles at the time but has since entered into a physically, mentally, and emotionally healthy semi-retirement. Bill was a multimillionaire many times over by the time that I met him. None of it was inherited or won in the lottery. It was all self-made.

Because of his stellar business success and reputation in the community, many people wanted a piece of his schedule and his attention. Some wanted his time to learn and grow. Some wanted to get him involved on their boards or committees. Some needed his direction and guidance from within the company. Still others wanted his financial contributions.

Basically, many people wanted his time and energy. It would have been very easy for him to become tired, burned out, or frustrated. Instead, he maintained his health and vitality. As a result, his efficiency and his effectiveness continued to grow and flourish in ways that many others only dream of.

As I recalled Bill, I remembered a conversation that we had while I was living in the Chicago area and growing our consulting business. I was intrigued by him, and like many others, wanted to learn from his stellar success. He and I served on the board of directors of a non-profit to which we both made contributions.

He had just rotated off as chairman of that board, and we were having lunch at the 410 Club in Chicago. It is a private club to which he belongs. We had enjoyed several lunches there in the past couple of years. Today we were discussing succession leadership for the board during his post-chairman tenure as a board member.

"Bill, I am absolutely intrigued by how you keep a balance in your life. I have known you for a couple of years now, and I continue to grow more amazed," I began.

"Thank you for the compliment," he said with a genuine, warm smile.

Bill is a very distinguished man. At the time, he was in his late fifties and had classic gray hair that complemented his seasoned experience. His shirts and suits were impeccable, a tribute to the careful nature with which he handled himself and his interactions. His shoes were so shiny you could use them to shave.

"I mean it, Bill," I continued. "I have a lot of respect for you for many reasons. Obviously you have done well in business and are very financially astute, but that isn't what I am referring to."

In his sophisticated and demure manner, he continued to listen as the waiter brought him his flavored iced tea and custom-made Cobb salad.

"Thank you," he greeted the waiter.

"Anything else, sirs?" the waiter inquired.

I was at the 410 Club. I wanted to say, "Yes, Monsieur, could you please pay off my mortgage and order me a Bentley? Put it on my tab." However, restraint from sharing such a socially inappropriate, although childishly funny comment was exactly what had earned me the right to be sitting with Bill at that moment. (Notice I said restraint from sharing, not from thinking. I always enjoy a good laugh even if it is only in my head.)

"That will be all," Bill said with his usual commanding presence. The waiter left and went to the next table.

Even though Bill was in his late fifties, he didn't have any middle-aged spread. He was as fit and trim as ever. His shirt was tucked into his suit just above an alligator-leather Gucci belt that matched his shoes. The belt revealed that he had taken exquisite care of his body and was more fit than many men half his age.

As he looked at me, inviting me to continue, I could not help but notice that he lacked that aged look that so many people, both his age and younger, display when they have been overworked and overstressed. He did not have the bags under his eyes that many others have when they have lost sleep on a regular basis. He did not have the lines of stress and worry on his face like so many who never took care of themselves first. He did not have the anxious look in his eyes of someone who feels the unrealistic demands and pressures of others caving in on them. He did not have any of this.

"Bill, if you were to sum up for me, a friendly acquaintance of yours who studies human potential for a career, the 'secret to your success,' what would that be?"

He paused and waited for me to finish my thought. We had known each other long enough that he realized I would not leave it that open-ended.

"Bill, it is no secret to you or me that many people half your age are not as fit as you, look more stressed than you, and still don't have the incredible lifestyle that you do. I admire you for that."

He smiled humbly, yet quietly proud as he looked down at his salad and moved the lettuce around with his fork to just where he wanted it. That was his way. Make decisions. Take action. Move quietly. Get things done. He was precise, right down to his Cobb salad.

"If you were to distill what you have learned and practiced into something that Julie and I could share with others, what would that be?" Now I left it open-ended.

He swallowed his salad and wiped his mouth with the grace of one who dines with presidents of countries, which he had. He took a sip of his tea and gently placed the glass on the table with the quietness of cotton linen. You would never know it was a crystal glass being set on a glass tabletop. That was his way. Decisive, yet wonderfully calculated right down to his lunch dining.

He folded his napkin and placed it back on his lap before he spoke. I had come to expect and appreciate his pregnant pauses. He was very methodical in the way he thought before he spoke.

"You must take the physical and emotional time and energy for yourself first if you are going to be even remotely successful at your endeavors in life," he said with the matter-of-factness of a man in his late fifties who has amassed a fortune.

I looked at him. My head moved slightly forward and my

eyebrows went slightly up as if to say with my body language, "Please continue."

"You must schedule time for yourself as paramount."

I baited him in a friendly manner. "Take time for yourself even before your family?" I asked almost rhetorically.

He smiled. "How can you be there for your family if you aren't there for yourself first?" he responded.

"Bill, how do you do that with so many people wanting your time and energy?" I inquired.

"You schedule it first. Nothing comes before it. Nothing." His response was not harsh, but gentle and sincere. "The more success you achieve in anything in life, money aside, the more people are going to want your time and energy. They want to know how you did it so that they can do it as well. They will take all that you can give them.

"They don't mean it in a mean way, for the most part; they really don't. Their world just revolves around themselves. That is human nature. It's not that they don't care that several other people want your time and energy at the same time. They don't even think that far ahead. They just know that they want your time and energy. Time and energy for yourself is the first part to maintaining the integrity of health."

"The integrity of health," I responded. "What a wonderful way to put it."

He paused, gracefully wiped the corners of his mouth with the linen napkin, and carefully placed it on his lap once again. "Well," he said and paused. "Think about what the word integrity means. It means 'the state of being whole.'"

I am having lunch with a walking dictionary, I thought to myself, but I remained silent to maintain the sophistication of this important moment.

"And," he continued, "health can be defined as 'soundness of body or mind.' So putting the two together, time and energy for yourself first is the key to maintaining the wholeness of your body and mind."

I was impressed. This is exactly what I expected and had hoped for. I was hearing the words of wisdom of someone who had mastered 'integrity of health' on both the physical and mental levels. "What else, Bill?" I invited.

"Beyond that, Chris, is schedule and routine."

I wasn't surprised that he said that. He lived north of Chicago in an affluent area, surrounded by retired actors and actresses, professional sports figures, and fellow millionaires. Chicago traffic can be brutal at rush hour, to put it mildly. As a result, people were often seen running to catch a train or cursing the fact that they were late and had missed it. Ironically, this is the example that he went into for his next point.

"I take the train in to work and home at night. I take the 7:05 in the morning to get to work by 8:00. I work through lunch, take the 4:30 train home, and get there at 5:30. I can read the *Wall Street Journal* on the way in and the daily paper on the way home."

"Bill," I said, recalling something else about him that greatly impressed me. "I have seen you arrive at work on at least a half-dozen occasions and have personally walked with you back to the train station at the end of the work day on as many occasions. I noticed something."

"What is that?" he asked, pausing and setting his fork on an angle on the side of his plate.

"I don't think that you use a briefcase."

"No, I don't."

"Why is that?"

"Because I don't need one."

I begged a moot point, "Why not?"

"For what?" he asked in rhetorical fashion, knowing where we were both headed.

"For paperwork," I stated.

"Work time is for work. Home time is for self and family," he said with utter confidence. He was right. I knew it, and he knew it. However, there was more to it than that. "Take care of yourself first, and you will have enough time to finish the things that you need to get done."

"What if you can't get it all done in that timeframe?" I asked knowing how he would respond.

"Then," he said, using one of his infamous pregnant pauses that seemed to say, "I suppose that everyone should know that, but since they don't, I will take the time to explain it so that they can come to my level," in a proud yet non-egotistical manner. "Then," he repeated after the pause, "you haven't taken care of yourself first by surrounding yourself with others to whom you can delegate."

"I see," I said, once again inviting the continuance.

"You can't do everything," he stated with no room for discussion. "You first must take care of yourself and what you need to do to maintain the integrity of your health. Then you must discipline yourself to be able to release the things that you may be able to do but that someone else could do. The chances are, many of the things that you can do, they cannot. As a result, you do what you do and delegate the rest."

"What if there is no one to delegate to?" I asked in circular logic.

"Then, as I said, you haven't put yourself first. If you truly want to surround yourself with people who can assist you, you *will* find a way." He said the word 'will' in a manner than meant there was no room for negotiation if you really meant it. "Okay, Bill," I proceeded, suspecting his answer, "won't some perceive it as selfish to put yourself first?" I asked.

"Those who don't understand the oxygen-mask theory would, I suppose. You give yourself the oxygen first on the airplane. It is the same way in life. If you never get beyond taking care of yourself to taking care of others, that is simply selfish. That is as much nonsense as only taking care of others and never taking care of yourself. You must put these things in order and reach a balance. Take care of yourself first, and then use that integrity of physical and mental health to take care of others."

"Then maintain discipline and a schedule, right?"

"Exactly," he said.

He made a lot of sense. He not only understood it; he was living it. He was the living epitome of his philosophy. As I pondered this, I realized that this would be the perfect ending for a book on personal excellence and high-performance leadership.

Bill had perfected personal excellence at a level that showed in his physical and emotional youth, and vibrancy in his late fifties. He had also perfected leadership in a way that made him personally, socially, and professionally successful.

As the stair stepper informed me that I was through, I wiped down the machine with a towel and headed for the showers. Now it was time to take these interactions and concepts and put them into practice.